The Ultimate
SLOW
COOKER
Cookbook

The Ultimate
SLOW
COOKER
Cookbook

Flavorful One-Pot Recipes for Your Crockery Pot

Carol Heding Munson

Sterling Publishing Co., Inc.
New York, New York

Food Stylists:
ROBERT WYSONG and **DAVID W. ROWLAND,**
Executive Sous Chefs at Grove Park Inn Resort, Asheville, NC

Art Director:
THERESA GWYNN

Photographer:
EVAN BRACKEN

Project Editor:
DAWN CUSICK

Assistant Editor and Production Assistant:
MEGAN KIRBY

Library of Congress Cataloging-in-Publication Data Available

3 5 7 9 10 8 6 4 2

Published by Sterling Publishing Company, Inc.
387 Park Avenue South
New York, N.Y. 10016

© 2001 by Carol Heding Munson

Distributed in Canada by Sterling Publishing,
c/o Canadian Manda Group, One Atlantic Ave., Suite 105
Toronto, Ontario, Canada M6K 3E7

Distributed in the U.K. by Guild of Master Craftsman Publications Ltd.,
Castle Place, 166 High Street, Lewes, East Sussex, England BN7 1XU
Tel: (+ 44) 1273 477374, Fax: (+ 44) 1273 478606,
Email: pubs@thegmcgroup.com, Web: www.gmcpublications.com

Distributed in Australia by Capricorn Link (Australia) Pty Ltd.,
P.O. Box 704, Windsor, NSW 2756, Australia

The recipes, written instructions, photographs, and illustrations in this volume are
intended for the personal use of the reader and may be reproduced for that purpose
only. Any other use, especially commercial use, is forbidden under law without written permission of the copyright holder.

Every effort has been made to ensure that all the information in this book is accu-
rate. However, due to differing conditions, tools, and individual skills, the publisher
cannot be responsible for any injuries, losses, and other damages that may result
from the use of the information in this book.

Manufactured in China

All rights reserved

Sterling ISBN 0-8069-7883-X

Table of Contents

Introduction

My situation is hardly unique: At the end of an 8- or 9-hour business day when I'm bushed and the family's hungry, there's nothing more rewarding than the aroma of a home-cooked meal. Even as I write this, I can hear the clamors: "What's for dinner? When do we eat?" Regardless of how busy our families are, though, everyone wants a nice meal. Fast-food takeout or something made in the microwave is fine every once in a while, but what everyone really wants is to sit down to a delicious, home-cooked meal. This book will show you the way to an incredible variety of wonderful, home-cooked meals that will fit into your busy schedule. The recipes for each presented here have all been designed to let you have a home-cooked meal waiting for you when you get home or shortly thereafter. And, after you've finished enjoying one of these great recipes, you'll enjoy the second benefit to one-pot cooking: easy clean up.

I have enjoyed cooking with a crockery pot, or slow cooker, for many years. Early in the day, when I feel fresh, I can toss a few ingredients into the slow cooker, then let it do its thing: simmer up a robust stew, or a light soup, or a flavorful pasta sauce. In the evening, when I'm ready to eat, dinner's done. As my success with this style of cooking grew, I wanted to share my best experiences with other cooking enthusiasts. What followed is this book, which is packed with quick-fix entrees, side dishes, and desserts.

These recipes are good for you—meaning low in fat and low in sodium. What's more, each has an incredible marriage of flavors that comes only from lengthy cooking. From the international favorites to the home-style dishes, every recipe that appears here had to pass muster not only with adults who enjoy gourmet foods, but also with my teenagers—independent critics with sharp taste buds and uninhibited opinions. Only the tastiest recipes survived. You should feel free to experiment with your own variations—who knows, you may even create enough favorite new combinations to fill your own cookbook. And along the way you'll experience another reward of slow cooking: the sensory pleasure of coming home to mouthwatering aromas.

This book features more than 200 great answers to that age-old question of "What's for dinner?" I hope you enjoy them all.

Carol Heding Munson

Slow Cooker Basics

Logical it isn't, practical it is: Crockery pot cooking makes for fast, great-tasting meals that suit your schedule. Here's how the process works. Early in the day, ingredients are prepared and go into an electric crockery pot, where they simmer and blend for three to eight unattended hours. Then, whenever you say, "Let's eat," a fabulous main event—entrée, stew, or soup—is ready for serving. The concept of crockery pot cooking has been around for centuries. Electric crockery pots became hot items in the early 1970s, but a decade or so later, many cooks considered them unsophisticated relics of a bygone era. Not so, say the crockery pot manufacturers. According to them, the handy appliances never really went out of style; millions of cooks (including me) continued to buy and use them for their intrinsic benefits. Now they're making a fashion comeback, and for good reasons! Why wait?

About Crockery Pots

The crockery pot is very energy efficient. When set to LOW, it actually draws less electricity than a 100-watt light bulb. The crockery pot, therefore, is economical to use and won't overheat the kitchen, even when simmering a roast for 10 to 12 hours. It also fits nicely on any countertop and stores handily in pantries as well.

Here are more reasons to take it slow: Gentle all-day simmering tenderizes lean meats and sturdy vegetables (carrots, rutabagas, potatoes, winter squash) for high-flavor, low-fat meals. And low cooking temperatures—200°F (93.3°C) when set on LOW; 300°F (149°C) on HIGH—mean that timing is flexible. A half-hour more or less won't spoil your meal.

Still more advantages: Most crockery pot recipes can be put together in 15 to 30 minutes. The cook need only measure and chop the ingredients, toss everything into the pot, and turn it on. (Some recipes also suggest sautéing meat, onions, or other ingredients before cooking for added flavor.) Several hours later, depending on the heat setting selected and the fullness of the pot, dinner's done. Could meal preparation get any easier or quicker? Well, perhaps, two meals for the work of one. Now, we're cooking! Depending on the size of the pot, crockery pots can handle food for a small crowd, so you can easily double small recipes or select ones that make 8 or 10 servings.

Cooker Styles

Crockery pots come in two basic shapes—round and rectangular—and in medium and large sizes that range from 3 to 6 quarts. Less common are mini 1- and 2-quart crockery pots. Most of the minis, which may be battery operated, are electric and are designed to work on standard household current. Cords are short, so units must be placed near outlets.

At the core of most round crockery pots is a heavy ceramic bowl, which may or may not be removable. The bowl is surrounded by a metal sheaf that encases electric heating coils. Rectangular crockery pots have a removable nonstick metal bowl (really more like a high-sided pan) that sits on a multi-purpose base, which encloses a heating element with a temperature selection dial. Depending on the model and price, both types can be bought with either snug-fitting glass or lightweight plastic lids. The plastic lids stay somewhat cooler to the touch, but may turn opaque if you use your cooker a lot.

Buying a new crockery pot? Check out seasonal sales at major chain stores for price discounts up to 50%. Be sure to get one with a removable bowl even if the whole thing costs a bit more. It's worth the few extra dollars. Why? You can submerge the bowl in water for easy washing. And you can stash it in the refrigerator if you've prepared ingredients beforehand. When you're ready to cook, simply return the bowl to the unit and turn the switch on. Both ceramic and metal bowls are oven-safe, although ceramic ones aren't broiler-safe and metal ones can't go in a microwave. Ceramic bowls aren't for stove-top use, either; any sautéing before cooking must be done in a skillet—a minor inconvenience.

The beauty of a crockery pot is its plug-and-cook feature: toss everything in the pot, switch it on, and let the pot do its cooking thing. But can it really go the distance unattended? Yes, for the most part. Experience indicates that some foods, such as pot roasts that cook for 10 hours, will occasionally stick in cookers that have bottom-only heating elements. An infrequent stir—once every two hours or so—takes care of the problem.

For even cooking, dishes that require very little liquid can benefit from a stir as well. About halfway through cooking, stir to reverse the ingredients on the top and those on the bottom. Enjoy experimenting with your crockery pot; recipes react differently to each one, depending on things like bowl size, type of crockery pot, heat setting, and food density.

When it comes to cooking times, expect differences. All crockery pots are not necessarily equal. The accuracy of a crockery pot's thermostat and the location of heating elements (surrounding a ceramic bowl or below a metal one) can speed or slow cooking by a couple of hours. Is one better than another? It's difficult to say, since other factors also come into play: voltage fluctuations, how cold food is at the start of cooking, how often the lid is picked up, how full the crockery pot is, and the density of ingredients. No matter which crockery pot you select—or already have—plan on adjusting recipe times and sometimes increasing or decreasing the heat. Play around with your cooker and you'll get to know its character.

Cooking Basics by Food Group

Is your appetite up for some seriously delicious slow cooking? The following guidelines will help smooth the transition from stove top to crockery pot cooking.

MEATS AND POULTRY

- Buy roasts in sizes and shapes that fit your cooker. Otherwise, you'll have to hunt up a meat cleaver and cut them to fit.

- Use lean cuts of meat and poultry for low-fat meals. Before cooking, trim away all visible fat and remove poultry skin.

- Brown ground beef, lamb, chicken, and turkey in a skillet over medium-high heat to give chilies, pasta sauces, and other dishes rich flavor and appealing dark color. To brown the low-fat way, use a nonstick skillet and mist it with a nonstick spray. After the meat is browned, transfer it to the slow cooker, using a slotted spoon so excess fat remains in the skillet.

- Cook cubed beef, chicken, pork, and turkey on LOW for up to 10 hours, but check them after 7 hours. They may be done. For added flavor, brown the cubes before putting them in the crockery pot.

- Add visual appeal and rich braised flavor by browning roasts before cooking them in the crockery pot.

VEGETABLES

- Place dense root vegetables, such as carrots, turnips, celery root, potatoes, onions, and rutabagas, on the pot bottom, and keep them submerged in the liquid for uniform cooking. Top vegetables with meat (though it's hard to believe, meat cooks faster than the root crops); pour liquids in last.

- Chop vegetables into consistent sizes for even cooking. Bite-size is always good, and ½"–2" sticks are attractive for Asian-style dishes.

- Stir in frozen peas, cut green beans, and mixed vegetables during the last 15 to 30 minutes of cooking if quantities are small (about ½ cup).

- Add tender vegetables (such as peas and snow peas); strongly flavored vegetables (such as broccoli, brussels sprouts, and cauliflower); and greens (such as kale, spinach, and escarole) during the last 15 to 60 minutes of cooking. Adding large quantities of last-minute goodies will temporarily lower the temperature of the cooking food. Timing depends on how much you're putting in.

- Brown onions and other vegetables to add caramelized color and flavor to dishes. Use the same low-fat techniques described for browning meats and poultry.

PASTA, RICE, AND OTHER GRAINS

- Use long-grain rices. In slow cooking, they give the fluffiest results.

- Stir in raw rice and barley during the last 1 to 1½ hours of cooking. All-day cooking would result in gummy, almost gelatinous and gloppy grains. Use an extra ¼ cup water for every ¼ cup of raw grain. Alternate solution: Cook grains by conventional stove-top and microwave methods; then stir them in during the last 15 minutes. Brown and wild rice buffs take note: The cooking time for brown rice is approximately twice that of white rice. Wild rice takes even longer than brown.

■ Add pasta to soups during the last 5 to 10 minutes of cooking. For other dishes, cook pasta on the stove top, then drain it, and top or toss it with the crockery pot ingredients right before serving. Whichever way it's cooked, pasta is best when done al dente.

DRIED BEANS

■ Cooking time varies with bean types and the ingredients cooked with them. Baby limas, great northern beans, and small white beans take less cooking than garbanzos (chick-peas) and kidney beans. Dried beans will roughly double their volume when cooked.

■ Boil garbanzo and red kidney beans with three times their volume of water in a large pot on the stove top for 10 minutes. Drain the beans in a colander and discard the water. Add the beans to other ingredients in the crockery pot.

■ Soften beans completely before combining them with sweeteners (including brown sugar, honey, maple syrup, and molasses) or acid foods (such as vinegar or tomatoes), which actually harden legumes during cooking. Here's an easy way to do it: Boil beans for 10 minutes, then reduce the heat, cover the pot, and allow the beans to simmer until they're tender, about 1½ hours. Discard the water. Add to ingredients in the crockery pot.

CHEESE, MILK, AND OTHER DAIRY PRODUCTS

■ Stir cheese, sour cream, yogurt, and cream into main dishes, soups, and stews right before serving. Then cook just long enough to melt the cheese and heat all the ingredients. If cooked for hours, dairy foods tend to separate and look curdled.

■ Opt for processed cheeses, which can tolerate heat fairly well, if you must cook cheese for a long period.

■ Add milk just before serving, except in dessert recipes created to cook in two to three hours. Milk curdles with lengthy cooking.

■ Try canned evaporated skim milk for the longest curdle-free cooking. In many dishes, it makes an excellent low-fat alternative to cream.

FISH

■ Stir in shellfish—minced clams, shrimp, scallops—during the last 15 to 60 minutes of cooking, depending on quantity. Shellfish toughens if cooked for long periods.

■ Mix in bite-size chunks of sturdy fish such as salmon and shark during the last 30 to 60 minutes of cooking. Cook until done. (To check for doneness, test the fish with a fork. Fully cooked fish should flake easily.)

■ Don't use delicate fish such as flounder. It won't hold up during lengthy cooking.

Secrets to Success

Okay, now you've had the basic course in slow cooking. What follows are eight other helpful hints for sure-fire crockery pot success.

▪ Adjust seasonings at the end of cooking. Some spices, such as black pepper, intensify with lengthy cooking. Others, such as basil and garlic, become diluted and less pungent. Rule of thumb, er…spice: Include whole spices at the beginning of cooking; stir in ground spices and tender herbs at the end. Before serving, taste your creation, and spice it up as desired.

▪ Garnish dishes for visual pizzazz. Colors fade with lengthy cooking, and a simple garnish can really brighten things up. Here's a handful of off-the-shelf suggestions:

> **Chopped, seeded tomatoes**
>
> **Crumbled bacon**
>
> **Dollop of sour cream, yogurt, or cottage cheese**
>
> **Fresh ground black or white pepper**
>
> **Grated cheese**
>
> **Ground nutmeg or ground paprika**
>
> **Slivered, sliced, or ground nuts**
>
> **Sprigs or snippings of parsley, cilantro, rosemary, thyme or other herbs**
>
> **Toasted croutons**
>
> **Wedges or slices of lemon, lime, or orange.**

▪ Use small quantities of liquids when cooking soups. Before serving, thin the soup to an appropriate consistency with water, broth, tomato juice, or milk. Cover and heat on HIGH until hot, 15 to 60 minutes.

▪ Jump-start cooking by setting the crockery pot on HIGH for the first hour.

▪ Resist peeking. Every time you lift the lid, cooking time is extended, because crockery pots aren't designed to crank up the heat when some escapes. These are slow, steady gizmos, from the start of cooking to the finish. Remove the lid only during the last half of cooking and do so only to stir food or check doneness.

▪ Prepare ingredients ahead, if you want, to make best use of your available time. But be certain to follow the food-safety suggestions in "Safety at Slow Speeds."

▪ Fill crockery pots half to three-quarters full, advise manufacturers. Refer to the instructions accompanying your crockery pot for more information.

▪ Increase cooking times as necessary if you live at a high altitude.

Safety at Slow Speeds

Food-safety experts assure us that cooking at low temperatures, 200°F (93.3°C) for LOW and 300°F (149°C) for HIGH, is completely safe if you follow these simple, common-sense guidelines:

1. Keep all perishable ingredients in the refrigerator until you're ready to start cooking.

2. Package raw meats and vegetables separately if you're preparing them ahead. You can place either meat or vegetables in the crockery pot bowl, cover, and refrigerate it, but don't mix the two until you're ready to cook.

3. Never partially cook meat or poultry and finish cooking it later. If you'll be sautéing or browning foods, do so right before adding them to the crockery pot and turning it on.

4. Check the doneness of roasts with a quick-read thermometer. In a matter of seconds, this handy little gadget will give you a read-out on the meat's internal temperature. The thermometers are available in most cook shops and many large supermarkets.

5. Avoid using large quantities of completely frozen foods in your crockery pot. It's fine to add up to a cup of frozen peas to a potful of hot soup, but starting a recipe with a pound of frozen beef cubes or a frozen turkey breast is a no-no. A crockery pot isn't designed to defrost foods; using it for that purpose can result in gastrointestinal woes. Avoid the risk: Always thaw foods in the refrigerator or microwave; then slow cook them.

6. Refrigerate leftovers quickly—certainly within two hours. If food has been on the table longer than that, don't take a chance. Throw it out. Bacteria thrive at room temperatures.

7. Never reheat foods in a crockery pot. For safety's sake, previously cooked foods should come to a boil quickly. Reheat on the stove top or in a microwave.

Kitchen Wisdom

Some of the following tips may seem obvious, and others may appear in the manufacturer's instruction booklet, but all bear repeating:

- Avoid sudden temperature changes. Really cold food or water can crack a hot ceramic bowl.

- Always use your crockery pot with the lid on. It's the only way slow cooking works!

- Don't immerse the heating elements in water.

- Turn off or unplug your crockery pot when you are done using it. (Some models have no on/off switch.)

Thickening Sauces and Gravies

Is your sauce or gravy thin and watery? That's common with many dishes, including slow-cooked ones. It's up to the cook to make them thick, rich, and smooth. Fortunately, thickening is easy once you know the techniques and the proper proportions of starchy thickener to liquid. For slow-cooked foods, any of the common thickeners work just fine. Choose arrowroot, cornstarch, flour, or tapioca. Here are the specifics on what to do.

Arrowroot and Cornstarch: At the end of cooking, turn the crockery pot to HIGH. For every 2 cups of liquid in the crockery pot, dissolve 2 tablespoons of arrowroot or cornstarch in 2 tablespoons of cold water in a measuring cup. Stir the arrowroot or cornstarch mixture into the food in the slow cooker. Cook for about 5 minutes until the gravy is thick. Don't overstir or overheat. Arrowroot breaks down with too much stirring; cornstarch does with too much heat.

Flour: At the end of cooking, turn the crockery pot to HIGH. For every 2 cups of liquid in the crockery pot, dissolve 4 tablespoons of instant or regular flour in 4 tablespoons of cold water in a measuring cup. Stir the flour mixture into the food in the crockery pot. Cook about 5 minutes until thick.

Tapioca: At the start of cooking, stir tapioca into the ingredients in the crockery pot. Use 3 to 4 tablespoons of tapioca for every 2 cups of liquid.

Other Thickeners: Potato flakes as well as mashed potatoes, pureed rice, and pureed beans make excellent thickeners. To thicken with them, follow the directions given with individual recipes.

Converting Family Favorites

Do you have some favorite soups, stews, and main dishes that you'd like to adapt to crockery pot cooking? Converting recipes is remarkably easy, almost failure-proof, if you follow the guidelines presented here. Read "Cooking Basics" and "Secrets to Success" earlier in this chapter. Apply the techniques discussed there, and make the following adjustments as well.

Liquid: When converting a recipe for slow cooking, reduce the amount of liquid by at least half that required in the conventional recipe. Why? Very little liquid escapes during slow cooking. In fact, condensation forms on the lid, drips back onto the food, and keeps everything nicely moist. A single cup of water, juice, or broth is usually plenty. For soups, use just enough broth or water to cover the ingredients.

Time: When going from stove-top speedy to slow-cooker steady cooking, allow plenty of simmering time. You'll need to experiment with each recipe, but this is the general conversion: Quadruple the conventional cooking time to get the slow-cooker time on LOW. Double the conventional cooking time to get the slow-cooker time on HIGH.

Healthful Cooking

Whether you're talking slow or conventional cooking, the best ways to decrease fat and sodium are to trim visible fat from meats; remove skin from poultry; add no salt; and cook with as little oil, butter, or margarine as possible.

For high-flavor, low-fat meals, use fatty foods, such as bacon, cheeses, sausage, and nuts in moderate portions. Just a little flavor from these foods can go a long way, as the recipes in this book demonstrate.

And to jazz up foods without salt, use liberal amounts of herbs and spices. Be sure to check the many fresh herbs and chilies available in today's supermarkets, and look for smoke flavorings in the spice section. Another neat trick: Use a couple teaspoons of wine vinegar to give many dishes a flavor boost without the actual sodium.

It's also important to select healthful, tasty alternatives to fatty, salty foods. Read nutritional labels on prepared foods; fats and sodium vary from brand to brand. Check the table on page 170, which lists some easy-to-find substitutes.

Flavor note: Salt hasn't been added to the recipes. If you prefer saltier flavors, feel free to add salt to taste. Just be aware that ¼ teaspoon of salt packs 533 milligrams (mg) of sodium. Consult the nutritional analysis for each recipe before modifying the amount of salt.

About the Nutritional Analyses

Many of the recipes in this book have a nutritional analysis, which gives today's inquisitive, diet-smart cook information about calories, fat, saturated fat, cholesterol, sodium, and dietary fiber. For most recipes, the analysis reflects a single serving. On an occasional sauce, it's for a specific amount, say ½ cup.

If a food is listed with a substitute ingredient, the analysis was figured using the first choice. For example, if a recipe lists ½ cup frozen peas or corn, the analysis was calculated on the peas. The analysis does not include optional ingredients, garnishes, or variations of ingredients. Analyses were calculated using Nutritionist IV (version 4) for Windows (First DataBank Division, The Hearst Corporation, 1995).

About the Ingredients

Many supermarkets stock seasonings like Thai spice, lemon grass, and 5-spice powder. Can't find them? If you live in a metropolitan area, try looking for them in Hispanic or Asian groceries. Live in a rural area? Consider phoning mail-order merchants listed in the back sections of many popular cooking and lifestyle magazines.

Low-Fat and Low-Sodium Choices

Choose This	To Replace That
Ground turkey breast meat	Ground beef or hamburger meat
Ground turkey breast meat	Ground turkey
Boneless, skinless chicken breasts	Chicken legs
Fat-free sour cream	Sour cream
Nonfat or low-fat yogurt	Sour cream, cream
Skim milk, evaporated skim milk, and 1% milk	Whole milk, cream
Reduced-fat Cheddar, Swiss, cheeses	Cheddar, Swiss, Monterey Jack cheeses
Fat-free or light cream cheese	Regular cream cheese
Beans (rinse and drain canned ones to remove as much sodium as possible)	Unrinsed, canned beans
Low-sodium tomato products	Regular tomato products
Fat-free, reduced-sodium broth (chicken and beef)	Regular chicken and beef broth
Low-sodium soy sauce	Regular soy sauce
Garlic powder	Garlic salt
Onion powder, dried minced onions	Onion salt
White wine vinegar, herbs, spices	Table salt

Special Stews

Beef Bourguignon

½ cup (70 g) flour

3 pounds (1.36 kg) beef rump roast, cut into 1-inch (2.5 cm) cubes

2 strips of bacon

1 teaspoon olive oil

6 tablespoons fat-free beef broth

1 package (16 ounces, 455 g) frozen pearl onions

½ cup (120 ml) Burgundy wine

Bouquet garni (celery stalk, thyme sprig, bay leaf, parsley sprig, and sage leaves, wrapped in cheesecloth)

Freshly ground black pepper

Like the classic French version, this rendition simmers beef in a hearty Burgundy wine, flavored with an aromatic bouquet garni. Serve over split baked potatoes, which soak up the wonderful broth, or dip into it with a side helping of crusty French bread.

MAKES 12 SERVINGS   **LARGE CROCKERY POT**

Place the flour in a clean paper bag, add the beef cubes, and gently shake the bag to coat them with the flour.

Cook the bacon in a nonstick skillet over medium-high heat until crisp, 3 to 5 minutes. Drain the strips on paper towels and crumble them. Using paper towels, wipe the skillet to remove excess fat.

Brown the beef in the same skillet over medium-high heat, adding the olive oil and broth as necessary to aid browning and to prevent sticking. Transfer the beef to the crockery pot.

In the same skillet as used before, quickly brown the onions, adding broth as needed to prevent sticking and to help loosen pieces of browned meat and flour. Cook for 1 to 2 minutes. Transfer the onions and pan scrapings to the crockery pot.

Stir in the Burgundy and add the bouquet garni. Sprinkle the beef and onion mixture with the pepper and crumbled bacon. Cover and cook on LOW until the meat and onions are tender, 8 to 10 hours. Discard the bouquet garni.

PER SERVING: About 218 calories, 6 g fat (25% of calories), 1.9 g saturated fat, 61 mg cholesterol, 135 mg sodium, 0.8 g dietary fiber.

COOK'S NOTES: To make a bouquet garni, tie fresh celery, thyme, bay leaf, parsley, and sage together with kitchen string. Or tie dried celery seed, thyme leaves, bay leaf, parsley flakes, and sage together in a small cheesecloth sack.

This dish freezes well for up to 1 month. To reheat, thaw it in the refrigerator, and cook until it's hot and bubbling throughout.

Superb Shrimp-and-Sausage Stew

1 medium potato, cut into ½-inch (13 mm) cubes

8 ounces (228 g) baby carrots

1 can (15 ounces, 426 g) baby corn, drained

1 large white onion, cut into thin wedges

½ cup (120 ml) fat-free chicken broth

1 can (16 ounces, 455 g) low-sodium stewed tomatoes

1 bay leaf

1 teaspoon chili powder

1 clove garlic, minced

½ pound (228 g) smoked sausage, cut in half lengthwise and sliced ½ inch (13 mm) thick

½ pound (228 g) medium shrimp, shelled and deveined

Succulent shrimp, richly flavored beef sausage, and whole baby vegetables make this robust stew especially attractive. Serve with crunchy slaw and hearty rye crisp bread.

MAKES 6 SERVINGS　　　　　　　　　**LARGE CROCKERY POT**

Combine the potatoes, carrots, corn, onions, broth, tomatoes, bay leaf, chili powder, and garlic in the crockery pot.

Brown the sausage in a nonstick skillet over medium heat. Transfer to the crockery pot, and stir to combine. Cover and cook on LOW for 8 to 10 hours.

During the last hour of cooking, stir in the shrimp. Cover and cook until the shrimp are done, about 1 hour. Discard the bay leaf.

PER SERVING: About 414 calories, 9.2 g fat (19% of calories), 0.3 saturated fat, 57 mg cholesterol, 464 mg sodium, 7.6 g dietary fiber.

COOK'S NOTE: Be sure to add the shrimp during the last hour of cooking, not sooner.

Thai-Spiced Pineapple and Pork Stew

1 pound (455 g) boneless pork loin chops, cut into ½-inch (13 mm) cubes

2 teaspoons canola oil

1 can (20 ounces, 570 g) pineapple chunks in juice, drained, juice reserved

Juice of 1 lime

2 teaspoons low-sodium soy sauce

1 tablespoon honey

1 teaspoon Thai seasoning

4 cloves garlic, slivered

1 sweet red pepper, cut into thin strips

1 pound (455 g) cherry tomatoes

1¼ cup (250 g) medium-grain rice

1 lime, thinly sliced

For the world-traveler within, a taste of Thailand's sweet-spicy cuisine at its finest. The cooking method is crockery-pot easy, of course.

MAKES 6 SERVINGS　　　　　　　　　**LARGE CROCKERY POT**

Brown the pork on all sides in the oil in a nonstick skillet over medium-high heat. Transfer the pork to the crockery pot.

Combine the reserved pineapple juice, lime juice, soy sauce, honey, Thai seasoning, and garlic in a 4-cup measure. Add enough water to equal 2 cups (480 ml). Mix well, and pour into the crockery pot.

Add the peppers and tomatoes. Cover and cook on HIGH for 3½ hours. Stir in the rice; add the lime slices. Cover and cook until the rice is tender and the liquid has been absorbed, about 1 hour.

PER SERVING: About 375 calories, 7 g fat (17% of calories), 1.9 g saturated fat, 40 mg cholesterol, 238 mg sodium, 1.6 g dietary fiber.

COOK'S NOTE: When adding the rice, stir the mixture gently so as not to split the tomatoes.

Ratatouille with Feta Cheese

1 cup (240 ml) fat-free beef broth

1 cup (200 g) crushed tomatoes

1 can (16 ounces, 455 g) stewed
    tomatoes

2 medium onions, halved and sliced

1 medium zucchini, thinly sliced

½ pound (228 g) eggplant, peeled and
    cut into ½-inch (13 mm) cubes

4 cloves garlic, minced

1 yellow pepper, thinly sliced

1 teaspoon white wine vinegar

2 sprigs of lemon thyme

6 leaves fresh basil, snipped

2 ounces (56 g) feta cheese, crumbled

*Mediterranean style: This old-world favorite is full to the brim
with eggplant and fresh basil flavors. Few dishes adapt better to
unattended slow cooking.*

MAKES 4 SERVINGS   **LARGE CROCKERY POT**

Combine the broth, tomatoes, and stewed tomatoes in the crockery
pot. Stir in the onions, zucchini, eggplant, garlic, pepper, and vinegar. Add the lemon thyme. Cover and cook on LOW for 6 to 8 hours
or on HIGH for 4 to 6 hours. Discard the lemon thyme and stir in
the basil. Divide the stew among 4 bowls and sprinkle feta cheese
over each serving.

PER SERVING: About 159 calories, 3.8 g fat (20% of calories), 2.2 g saturated fat, 12 mg cholesterol, 528 mg sodium, 3.4 g dietary fiber.

COOK'S NOTE: No lemon thyme available? Substitute a sprig of thyme and
a strip of lemon peel.

Old-Fashioned Pound Stew

1 pound (455 g) lean beef cubes

¼ cup (35 g) unbleached flour

½ teaspoon olive oil

1 pound (455 g) carrots, cut diagonally
    into 1-inch-thick (2.5 cm) pieces

1 pound (455 g) potatoes, cut into
    1-inch (2.5 cm) cubes

1 pound (455 g) plum tomatoes,
    chopped

1 pound (455 g) frozen pearl onions

⅛ teaspoon black pepper

1¼ cups (300 ml) water

2 cups (300 g) frozen peas

BASIC WHEAT DUMPLINGS
    (see page 158)

3 teaspoons browning sauce

2 tablespoons cornstarch

*Here's a simple, home-style stew like grandmom used to make. It uses
a pound (455 g) each of carrots, potatoes, onions, tomatoes, and beef.*

MAKES 8 SERVINGS   **LARGE CROCKERY POT**

Dredge the beef in the flour, then brown the pieces on all sides in
the oil in a nonstick skillet over medium-high heat, about 5 minutes. Transfer the beef to the crockery pot. Add the carrots, potatoes, tomatoes, pearl onions, pepper, and 1 cup (240 ml) of water;
mix. Cover and cook on LOW until the vegetables and beef cubes
are tender, 8 to 10 hours. Stir in the peas. Cover and and cook for
15 minutes.

Turn the heat to HIGH, and drop in the dumplings. Cover and cook
until they're done, about 30 minutes. Transfer the dumplings to a
plate and keep them warm.

In a measuring cup, mix the cornstarch, the remaining ¼ cup (60 ml)
of water, and browning sauce. Pour it into the stew, mix well, and
heat until the liquid is thickened. Serve the stew over the dumplings.

PER SERVING: About 238 calories, 3.4 g fat (13% of calories), 1 g saturated
fat, 30 mg cholesterol, 177 mg sodium, 5.2 g dietary fiber.

COOK'S NOTE: If pearl onions aren't available, use yellow onions and cut
them into wedges.

RATATOUILLE WITH FETA CHEESE

Garbanzo Chili with Ham and Peppers

¼ pound (114 g) thinly sliced tavern ham, chopped

1 can (28 ounces, 800 g) crushed tomatoes

1 can (15 ounces, 426 g) garbanzo beans (chick peas), rinsed and drained

1 can (14 ounces, 400 g) pinto beans, rinsed and drained

1 large onion, chopped

2 green bell peppers, chopped

½ cup (120 ml) water

2 tablespoons chili powder

1 tablespoon cider vinegar

1 teaspoon cumin seeds

6 cloves garlic, minced

1 dried cayenne pepper, seeded and minced

1 small avocado, diced, for garnish

Chase the chills with this stimulating chili, which makes for a hot, hearty meal anytime. To moderate the heat, use half a cayenne pepper and less chili powder, and serve with fat-free sour cream.

MAKES 8 SERVINGS　　　　　　　　　**LARGE CROCKERY POT**

Combine the ham, tomatoes, garbanzo beans, pinto beans, onion, bell peppers, water, chili powder, vinegar, cumin seeds, garlic, and cayenne pepper in the crockery pot. Cover and cook on LOW or HIGH until the vegetables are tender, and the flavors are blended, 4 to 6 hours on LOW or 3 to 4 hours on HIGH.

PER SERVING: 268 calories, 6.4 g fat, 644 mg sodium, 11.2 g dietary fiber.

QUICK TIPS: Wear gloves when seeding and chopping chilies. The compound responsible for their heat can sting and burn your fingers. Dip cut avocado in lemon or lime juice to slow browning, or oxidation.

Chicken with Sun-Dried Tomatoes

2 teaspoons olive oil

¾ pound (340 g) boneless, skinless chicken breast, cut into 1-inch (2.5 cm) cubes

1 leek, white part only, thinly sliced

2 shallots, chopped

1 teaspoon Italian herb seasoning

1 large potato, peeled and cubed

1 rib celery, sliced

½ cup, 28 g) diced sun-dried tomatoes

1 cup (200 g) crushed tomatoes

1 cup (240 ml) fat-free chicken broth

¼ cup (60 ml) dry red wine

Parsley sprigs, for garnish

Use dry-pack sun-dried tomatoes for wonderful, intense flavor. The tomatoes are dominant in this recipe, and they provide a surprising hint of sweetness.

MAKES 4 SERVINGS　　　　　　　　**MEDIUM CROCKERY POT**

Heat the oil in a large skillet over medium-high heat. Add the chicken, leek, shallots and Italian herb seasoning. Sauté, stirring occasionally, until the chicken is lightly browned, 5 to 10 minutes.

Combine the potatoes, celery, sun-dried tomatoes, chicken mixture, crushed tomatoes, broth, and wine in the crockery pot. Cover and cook on LOW until the potatoes are tender, the chicken is cooked through, and the flavors are blended, 6 to 8 hours. Serve garnished with the parsley.

PER SERVING: 308 calories, 5.7 g fat, 419 mg sodium, 3.8 g dietary fiber.

Bratwurst and Sweet Pepper Stew

1 teaspoon olive oil

¼ pound (114 g) cooked bratwurst, cut in half lengthwise and thickly sliced

1 large onion, sliced

3 carrots, sliced diagonally ¾ inch (20 mm) thick

2 large potatoes, cut into ½-inch (13 mm) cubes

2 ribs celery, sliced

1 large red bell pepper, thinly sliced

8 cloves garlic, thinly sliced

1 cup (240 ml) fat-free beef broth

1 cup (240 ml) nonalcoholic beer

¼ teaspoon freshly ground black pepper

1 teaspoon dried tarragon leaves

Take a quick trip to a bier halle in festive Munich—without leaving your kitchen and its familiar warmth. And savor this sturdy stew; it's brimming with flavorful vegetables and bratwurst, a German pork and veal sausage seasoned with ginger, nutmeg and coriander.

MAKES 4 SERVINGS　　　　　**MEDIUM CROCKERY POT**

Heat the oil in a nonstick skillet over medium-high heat. Add the bratwurst and onions, and sauté, stirring occasionally, until the onions are lightly browned, about 8 minutes.

Combine the bratwurst mixture, carrots, potatoes, celery, red peppers, garlic, broth, beer, black pepper, and tarragon in the crockery pot. Cover and cook on LOW until the vegetables are tender, the bratwurst is cooked through, and the flavors are blended, 6 to 8 hours.

PER SERVING: 272 calories, 8.9 g fat, 238 mg sodium, 5.5 g dietary fiber.

QUICK TIP: If bratwurst is unavailable, substitute kielbasa, a flavorful (and readily available) Polish sausage.

Spicy Three-Bean Stew

1 can (28 ounces, 800 g) whole plum tomatoes, cut up

1 can (15 ounces, 426 g) red kidney beans, rinsed and drained

1 can (15 ounces, 426 g) black beans, rinsed and drained

1 can (15 ounces, 426 g) pinto beans, rinsed and drained

1 cup (142 g) corn

½ cup (100 g) brown rice

6 cloves garlic, chopped

3 medium onions, quartered and separated

2 medium sweet red peppers, cut into thin strips

1 tablespoon chili powder

1 teaspoon ground cumin

¼ teaspoon ground allspice

¼ teaspoon ground coriander

1 tablespoon red wine vinegar

Fabulous flavor and lots of fiber characterize this vegetarian main course. It's a meal in itself.

MAKES 8 SERVINGS　　　　　**LARGE CROCKERY POT**

Combine the tomatoes, beans, corn, rice, garlic, onions, red peppers, chili powder, cumin, allspice, coriander, and vinegar in the crockery pot. Cover and cook on LOW for 7 to 9 hours or on HIGH for 4 to 6 hours.

PER SERVING: About 307 calories, 1.7 g fat (4% of calories), 0.3 g saturated fat, 0 mg cholesterol, 214 mg sodium, 12.1 g dietary fiber.

COOK'S NOTE: This hearty stew can be frozen for a week or two. After that, its spicy punch diminishes.

Savory Kielbasa–Potato Stew

½ pound (228 g) cooked turkey kielbasa, thinly sliced

1 pound (455 g) red potatoes, diced

1 onion, cut into thin wedges

1 rib celery, sliced

2 cups (240 ml) water

2 packets low-sodium beef bouillon powder (or 2 teaspoons bouillon granules)

¼ teaspoon freshly ground black pepper

½ teaspoon dried savory

1 cup (150 g) frozen peas, thawed

This hearty pairing of Polish sausage and red potatoes is low in calories, high in flavor, and will appeal to any appetite. Green peas add a splash of bright color.

MAKES 4 SERVINGS   **MEDIUM CROCKERY POT**

Cook the kielbasa in a nonstick skillet over medium-high heat, stirring occasionally, until lightly browned, about 8 minutes.

Combine the kielbasa, potatoes, onions, celery, water, bouillon, pepper, and savory in the crockery pot. Cover and cook on LOW or HIGH until the vegetables are tender, 5 to 7 hours on LOW or 3 to 5 hours on HIGH.

Stir in the peas, and recover the pot. Cook the stew until the peas are crisp-tender, about 5 minutes.

PER SERVING: 226 calories, 2.6 g fat, 417 mg sodium, 5.2 g dietary fiber.

QUICK TIP: Two cups (480 ml) fat-free store-bought beef broth can replace the water and bouillon. Just be aware that the dish will have more sodium.

Grecian Beef Stew

2 teaspoons olive oil

1 pound (455 g) beef rump roast, cut into thin ¾-inch-wide (20 mm), 2-inch-long (5 cm) strips

2 cups crushed tomatoes

2 onions, cut into thin wedges

1 eggplant (about 12 ounces, 340 g), peeled and cubed

¼ cup (60 ml) dry red wine

4 cloves garlic, minced

Juice of 1 lemon

1 tablespoon brown sugar

½ teaspoon ground cinnamon

⅛ teaspoon ground nutmeg

8 ounces (228 g) thin egg noodles

1 tablespoon crumbled feta cheese, for garnish

1 tablespoon chopped fresh mint leaves, for garnish

Cinnamon, nutmeg, and lemon give this tomato–beef stew its captivating Greek accent. Serve with a tossed greens salad to make a complete meal.

MAKES 4 SERVINGS   **MEDIUM CROCKERY POT**

Heat the oil in a large skillet over medium-high heat. Add the beef and onions and sauté, stirring occasionally, until the beef is lightly browned and the onions are translucent, 6 to 8 minutes.

Combine the beef mixture, tomatoes, eggplant, wine, garlic, lemon juice, sugar, cinnamon, and nutmeg in the crockery pot. Cover and cook on LOW until the beef is tender, 8 to 10 hours.

Cook the noodles, according to package directions. Drain well and divide among 4 plates. Top with the meat–eggplant mixture. Garnish each serving with the feta and mint.

PER SERVING: 520 calories, 8.4 g fat, 386 mg sodium, 7.3 g dietary fiber.

QUICK TIP: For maximum spicy flavor, use freshly grated nutmeg.

SAVORY KIELBASA–POTATO STEW

Teriyaki Beef with Broccoli

Nonstick spray

1 pound (455 g) beef rump roast, cut into thin ¾- x 2-inch (20 mm x 5 cm) strips

4 carrots, cut into 2-inch-long (5 cm) sticks

1 package (20 ounces, 570 g) frozen pearl onions

1 can (14 ounces, 420 ml) fat-free beef broth

2 tablespoons low-sodium teriyaki sauce

½ cup (120 ml) water

½ pound (228 g) broccoli florets

8 ounces (228 g) thin or medium noodles

This Asian-style dish is easy to make and fairly bursting with teriyaki's ginger-garlic flavor.

MAKES 4 SERVINGS　　　　　　　**MEDIUM CROCKERY POT**

Coat a nonstick skillet with garlic-flavored nonstick spray, and sauté the beef over medium-high until browned, about 5 minutes. Transfer the beef to the crockery pot.

Add the carrots, onions, broth, 1 tablespoon of teriyaki sauce, and water. Cover and cook on LOW until the meat is tender, 4 to 6 hours (or on HIGH, 7 to 9 hours). In the last half-hour, cook the noodles separately and drain them; keep warm.

Meanwhile, stir the broccoli into the beef mixture. Cover and cook until the broccoli is crisp-tender, about 5 minutes. Divide the noodles among 4 plates. Top with the beef mixture, and sprinkle with the remaining teriyaki.

PER SERVING: About 516 calories, 7.7 g fat (13% of calories), 2 g saturated fat, 60 mg cholesterol, 637 mg sodium, 6.1 g dietary fiber.

COOK'S NOTE: If reduced-fat canned broth isn't available, use the regular version and defat it. Here's what to do: Refrigerate the broth (unopened) for about 3 hours. The fat will rise to the top and congeal. Open the can and skim off the fat.

Home-Style Chicken Stew with Mushrooms and Peppers

1 teaspoon olive oil

1 onion, sliced

1½ cups (115 g) sliced mushrooms

1 pound (455 g) boneless, skinless chicken breast, cut into 1-inch (2.5 cm) cubes

1 can (14 ounces, 400 g) sliced stewed tomatoes

3 cups cubed acorn or butternut squash

4 cloves garlic, minced

2 bay leaves

¼ teaspoon freshly ground black pepper

½ cup (106 g) chopped roasted red peppers

Here's a easy stew with plenty of home-style flavor from mushrooms, tomatoes, squash, and roasted peppers. A tasty spinoff: Make with cubed pork or turkey breast instead of the chicken.

MAKES 4 SERVINGS　　　　　　　**MEDIUM CROCKERY POT**

Heat the oil in a large nonstick skillet over medium-high heat. Add the onions, mushrooms, and chicken and sauté, stirring occasionally, until the onions are translucent and the chicken is lightly browned, about 8 minutes.

Combine chicken mixture, tomatoes, squash, garlic, bay leaves, black pepper, and red peppers in the crockery pot. Cover and cook on LOW until the chicken is cooked through and the vegetables are tender, 6 to 8 hours. Discard the bay leaves.

PER SERVING: 291 calories, 5.5 g fat, 111 mg sodium, 6.8 g dietary fiber.

QUICK TIP: To save time, use roasted peppers from a jar.

Asian Stir-Fry Stew

1 cup (240 ml) Oriental broth, chicken, or vegetable broth

2 medium carrots, cut into ½-inch (13 mm) cubes

1 tablespoon minced gingerroot

1 clove garlic, minced

1 can (15 ounces, 426 g) baby corn, drained

1 cup (80 g) sliced scallions

1 can (8 ounces, 228 g) sliced water chestnuts

1 can (14 ounces, 400 g) bean sprouts

½ pound (228 g) bok choy, chopped

½ pound (228 g) bay scallops

1 teaspoon sesame oil

10 ounces (284 g) Chinese wheat noodles

Low-sodium soy sauce (optional)

1 tablespoon powdered hot mustard (optional)

When you want the flavor of a stir-fry, but not the last-minute fuss, give this easily prepared stew a try.

MAKES 4 SERVINGS   **MEDIUM CROCKERY POT**

Mix the broth, carrots, gingerroot, garlic, corn, scallions, chestnuts, and bean sprouts in the crockery pot. Cover and cook on LOW for 5 hours. Add the bok choy. Cover and cook for 15 minutes. Stir in the scallops and sesame oil. Cover and cook until the scallops are done, about 30 minutes. Boil the noodles in water and drain. Serve the stew over the noodles. Sprinkle with the optional soy sauce. Serve with the **hot mustard** for dipping, if you wish.

PER SERVING: About 467 calories, 6 g fat (10% of calories), 1 g saturated fat, 78 mg cholesterol, 474 mg sodium, 7 g dietary fiber.

COOK'S NOTE: To make **HOT MUSTARD,** combine 1 tablespoon powdered mustard with enough cold water to make a paste. Let the mixture stand for 10 minutes; then use with caution. This mustard packs the power to scorch your sinuses!

Hickory Steak Stew with Winter Vegetables

1 teaspoon olive oil

¾ pound (340 g) top round beef steak, cut into 1-inch (2.5 cm) cubes

1 large onion, chopped

4 cloves garlic, minced

1 can (14 ounces, 420 ml) fat-free beef broth

¼ cup (60 ml) hickory-flavored barbecue sauce

1 spaghetti squash (about 2 pounds, 910 g), peeled, seeded, and cut into 2-inch (5 cm) cubes

2 parsnips, peeled and sliced

2 russet potatoes, peeled and quartered

This simple stew has an unusual twist: spaghetti squash replaces the more common acorn or butternut variety. Serve with crusty bread to sop up the flavorful broth.

MAKES 4 SERVINGS   **MEDIUM CROCKERY POT**

Heat the oil in a large nonstick skillet over medium-high heat. Add the beef and sauté, stirring occasionally, just until browned, 5 to 7 minutes. Add the onions and garlic and sauté, stirring, just until the onions begin to brown.

Combine the beef mixture, broth, barbecue sauce, squash, parsnips, and potatoes in the crockery pot. Cover and cook on LOW until the beef and potatoes are tender, 8 to 10 hours.

PER SERVING: 411 calories, 6.9 g fat, 353 mg sodium, 10.6 g dietary fiber.

QUICK TIP: Use a sturdy chef's knife to peel and chop the spaghetti squash, which has a hard, shell-like skin.

Country-Style Chicken Stew Provençal

2 teaspoons olive oil

1 pound (455 g) boneless, skinless chicken breast, cut into 1-inch (2.5 cm) pieces

4 ounces (114 g) portobello mushrooms, cubed

1 can (14 ounces, 420 ml) fat-free chicken broth

¼ cup (60 ml) dry white wine

3 potatoes, sliced

1 can (15 ounces, 426 g) great northern beans, rinsed and drained

4 carrots, sliced

8 cloves garlic, minced

¼ teaspoon white pepper

1 teaspoon herbes de Provence

¼ cup (20 g) snipped fresh parsley, for garnish

Rustic stews like this one are loaded with sturdy vegetables and flavorful herbs. Enjoy carrots, potatoes, white beans, and mushrooms steeped in the special flavors of garlic and herbes de Provence.

MAKES 4 SERVINGS   **MEDIUM CROCKERY POT**

Heat the oil in a large nonstick skillet over medium-high heat. Add the chicken and mushrooms, and sauté, stirring occasionally, until the chicken is lightly browned, about 8 minutes.

Combine the chicken mixture, broth, wine, potatoes, beans, carrots, garlic, and white pepper in the crockery pot. Cover and cook on LOW until the chicken is cooked through, the potatoes are tender, and the flavors are blended, 6 to 8 hours.

Season with the herbes de Provence and serve garnished with the parsley.

PER SERVING: 477 calories, 7.2 g fat, 190 mg sodium, 12 g dietary fiber.

QUICK TIP: Save time by simply scrubbing, and not peeling, the potatoes.

Moroccan Lamb Stew with Couscous

1 pound (455 g) lean ground lamb

⅓ cup (27 g) quick oats

⅓ cup (27 g) dried parsley

⅓ cup dried minced onion

½ teaspoon ground coriander

⅛ teaspoon black pepper

⅛ teaspoon ground cinnamon

⅛ teaspoon ground nutmeg

4 cloves garlic, minced

½ teaspoon cumin seed

1 dried cayenne pepper, minced

2 pounds (910 g) tomatoes, chopped

½ cup (130 g) chopped dried apricots

½ cup (85 g) dried currants

1 cup (120 g) couscous

This palate-pleasing North African stew features coriander-seasoned meatballs in a tomato-apricot-currant sauce—an intriguing blend of bold spices and sweet fruit.

MAKES 12 SERVINGS   **LARGE CROCKERY POT**

Combine the lamb, oats, parsley, onions, coriander, pepper, cinnamon, and nutmeg. Shape into 1- x 2-inch meatballs, and brown in a nonstick skillet over medium-high heat.

Mix the garlic, cumin, cayenne, tomatoes, apricots, and currants in the crockery pot. Add the meatballs, cover, and cook on LOW until the lamb is cooked through and the apricots are tender, 7 to 9 hours. In a saucepan, bring 2 cups (480 ml) of water to a boil; stir in the couscous. Cover and remove from heat and allow to stand for 5 minutes. Serve stew over the hot couscous.

PER SERVING: About 178 calories, 3.3 g fat (16% of calories), 1.1 g saturated fat, 26 mg cholesterol, 33 mg sodium, 5.1 g dietary fiber.

COUNTRY-STYLE CHICKEN STEW PROVENÇAL

Winter Vegetable Stew with Cheddar and Croutons

1 potato, cut into ½-inch (13 mm) cubes

1 turnip, cut into ½-inch (13 mm) cubes

2 carrots, diagonally sliced ½ inch (13 mm) thick

1 celery stalk, diagonally sliced ½ inch (13 mm) thick

1 leek, white part only, sliced ½ inch (13 mm) thick

1 can (14 ounces, 420 ml) fat-free chicken broth

1 teaspoon dried savory

¼ teaspoon black pepper

¼ pound (114 g) broccoli florets

3 cups toasted croutons

1 cup (85 g) shredded Cheddar cheese

Bacon-flavored bits, for garnish

A hearty, flavorful stew for healthy appetites. And it's vitamin A-okay, courtesy of the carrots and broccoli.

MAKES 4 SERVINGS   **LARGE CROCKERY POT**

Combine the potatoes, turnips, carrots, celery, leek, broth, savory, and pepper in the crockery pot. Cover and cook on LOW until the vegetables are tender, 7 to 9 hours (or on HIGH for 4 to 6 hours).

Add the broccoli. Cover and cook until the broccoli is tender, about 15 minutes. Divide the stew among 4 bowls; top each serving with croutons, cheese, and bacon-flavored bits.

PER SERVING: About 320 calories, 11 g fat (30% of calories), 6.3 g saturated fat, 30 mg cholesterol, 604 mg sodium, 3.8 g dietary fiber.

COOK'S NOTE: To make **toasted croutons,** cut 3 slices of crusty bread into ½-inch cubes. Spread the cubes on a baking sheet or perforated pizza pan. Mist the cubes with nonstick spray, then broil them until they're golden, about 5 minutes. Shake or stir cubes to expose the uncooked sides; broil them until golden, about 3 minutes.

Hungarian-Style Goulash

Nonstick spray

2 pounds (910 g) beef rump roast, trimmed of fat and cut into 1½-inch (4 cm) cubes

6 medium onions, halved lengthwise and thinly sliced

2 cups (228 g) chopped portobello mushrooms

½ cup (120 ml) water

1 tablespoon paprika

¼ teaspoon black pepper

1 teaspoon browning sauce

2½ cups diced tomatoes or 1 can (14 ounce, 400 g) crushed tomatoes

16 ounces (455 g) broad noodles

Caraway seeds, for garnish

Known as gulyás in its native Hungary, this stew releases tantalizing aromas as browned beef simmers in a spicy mixture of mushrooms, onions, tomatoes and paprika. Serve with a simple green salad or steamed peas.

MAKES 8 SERVINGS   **LARGE CROCKERY POT**

Coat a nonstick skillet with nonstick spray, and warm it over medium heat. Add the beef and cook it until well-browned on all sides, 4 to 6 minutes. Transfer the beef to the crockery pot.

Add the onions and mushrooms to the same skillet, and sauté them until the onions are translucent, 3 to 5 minutes. Transfer the onion-mushroom mixture to the crockery pot. Pour the water into the skillet and bring it to a boil, scraping the skillet to remove the brown drippings.

Pour the liquid into the crockery pot. Add the paprika, pepper, browning sauce and tomatoes to the crockery pot. Mix well. Cover and cook on LOW until the beef is tender, 8 to 10 hours. When the goulash is done, boil the noodles in water and drain. Serve the goulash over hot noodles and garnish each serving with a sprinkling of caraway.

PER SERVING: About 364 calories, 10 g fat (25% of calories), 3.2 g. saturated fat, 101 mg cholesterol, 210 mg sodium, 4.1 g dietary fiber.

COOK'S NOTES: Goulash, minus the noodles, can be frozen for up to a month. To reheat, thaw it in the refrigerator, and cook until it's hot and bubbly throughout.

Keep leftover noodles for just a day or two in the refrigerator. Refresh them in boiling water.

Chicken, Carrot, and Apple Stew

2 teaspoons olive oil

¾ pound (339 g) boneless, skinless chicken breast, cut into ¾-inch (20 mm) cubes

1 large onion, cut into thin wedges

1 can (14 ounces, 420 ml) fat-free chicken broth

½ cup (80 g) dark raisins

2 carrots, sliced ¼-inch (6 mm) thick

1 russet potato, cut into ½-inch (13 mm) cubes

½ cup (90 g) baby lima beans

1 Rome apple, chopped

1 teaspoon brown sugar

¼ teaspoon celery seeds

½ teaspoon curry powder

⅛ teaspoon ground turmeric

2 tablespoons precooked cornmeal, such as Masarepa®

1 teaspoon Louisiana hot sauce

At the end of a busy day, enjoy this sensational dish that mixes sweet (apples and raisins) with spicy (curry, turmeric, and hot-pepper sauce).

MAKES 4 SERVINGS **MEDIUM CROCKERY POT**

Heat the oil in a large nonstick skillet over medium-high heat. Add the chicken and onions, and sauté, stirring occasionally, until browned, 4 to 6 minutes.

Remove the chicken mixture to the crockery pot. Stir in the broth, raisins, carrots, potato, lima beans, apple, sugar, celery seeds, curry, and turmeric. Cover and cook on LOW until the potatoes are tender, the chicken is cooked through, and the flavors are blended, 6 to 8 hours. Stir in the Masarepa and hot sauce.

PER SERVING: 430 calories, 6.1 g fat, 222 mg sodium, 10.1 g dietary fiber.

QUICK TIP: Other varieties of apple — Cortland, Empire, Golden Delicious, Granny Smith, Macintosh, and Winesap — can be substituted for the Rome apple.

RUSTIC CHICKEN STEW

Rustic Chicken Stew

2 pounds (910 g) boneless, skinless
    chicken breasts, cut into
    1-inch (2.5 cm) cubes

3 medium onions, quartered

2 carrots, cut into 1-inch-thick
    (2.5 cm) slices

2 potatoes, cut into 1-inch
    (2.5 cm) cubes

2 cans (14 ounces, 420 ml) each),
    fat-free chicken broth

1 teaspoon celery seed

1 teaspoon dried thyme leaves

½ teaspoon black pepper

8 ounces mushrooms, halved

1 cup (150 g) frozen corn

1 cup (150 g) frozen peas

This chunky stew is easy to make and features chicken, carrots, corn, and peas—all tastefully seasoned with thyme.

MAKES 8 SERVINGS   **LARGE CROCKERY POT**

Combine the chicken, onions, carrots, potatoes, and broth in the crockery pot. Stir in the celery seed, thyme, pepper, mushrooms, and corn. Cover and cook on LOW until the chicken is done and the vegetables are tender, 7 to 9 hours (or on HIGH 4 to 6 hours). Stir in the peas and cook until they're done, 15 to 30 minutes.

PER SERVING: About 295 calories, 4.6 g fat (14% of calories), 1.2 g saturated fat, 96 mg cholesterol, 249 mg sodium, 3.4 g dietary fiber.

COOK'S NOTE: Baby carrots make a quick and easy substitute for the 1-inch-thick carrot slices.

Shrimp and Mako Shark Gumbo

1 medium onion, finely chopped

2 celery stalks, thinly sliced

1 teaspoon butter

1 can (14 ounces, 420 ml) fat-free
    chicken broth

1 sweet green pepper, chopped

8 ounces (228 g) okra, sliced, or 1
    package (10 ounces, 284 g) frozen

2 cloves garlic, minced

1 can (28 ounces, 800 g) whole
    tomatoes, cut up

½ teaspoon Louisiana hot sauce,
    or to taste

2 bay leaves

½ pound (228 g) medium shrimp,
    shelled and deveined

½ pound (228 g) mako shark steak, cut
    into 1-inch (2.5 cm) cubes

2¼ cups (450 g) rice

Gumbo wouldn't be gumbo without okra, the king of vegetables in bayou country. Our easy-cooking gumbo uses mako shark, but you can substitute catfish, if you wish.

MAKES 6 SERVINGS   **LARGE CROCKERY POT**

Sauté the onions and celery in the butter in a nonstick skillet over medium-high heat until translucent. Transfer the vegetables to the crockery pot.

Stir in the broth, green peppers, okra, garlic, tomatoes, hot sauce, and bay leaves. Cover and cook on LOW for 7 to 9 hours or on HIGH for 3½ to 5 hours. In the last half-hour, cook the rice separately; keep it warm.

Meanwhile, gently stir the shrimp and mako into the gumbo in the crockery pot. Cover and cook on HIGH until the shrimp and mako are cooked through, 30 to 60 minutes. Serve over the hot cooked rice.

PER SERVING: About 412 calories, 4.1 g fat (9% of calories), 1.1 g saturated fat, 78 mg cholesterol, 225 mg sodium, 3.7 g dietary fiber.

Sausage and Butternut Squash Stew

1½ pound (680 g) butternut squash, peeled and cut into ½-inch (13 mm) cubes

1 medium potato, cut into ½-inch (13mm) cubes

2 slender carrots, sliced diagonally ½-inch (13 mm) thick, or 12 baby carrots

1 cup (150 g) frozen cut green beans

1 can (14 ounces, 420 ml) fat-free beef broth

1 tablespoon red wine vinegar

¼ teaspoon black pepper

1 teaspoon dried rosemary, crushed

¼ pound (114 g) low-fat turkey sausage or light kielbasa, cut in half lengthwise and thickly sliced

4 small onions, halved

¼ cup (60 ml) cold water

2 tablespoons cornstarch

Snipped fresh parsley, for garnish

This deliciously earthy stew is great for chasing the chills on a nippy fall day. Serve with slices of hearty oat bread.

MAKES 4 SERVINGS   **MEDIUM CROCKERY POT**

Combine the squash, potatoes, carrots, beans, broth, vinegar, pepper, and rosemary in the crockery pot.

Brown the sausage in a skillet over medium-high heat; add the onions and cook until the onions are lightly browned, about 4 minutes. Transfer the sausage and onions to the crockery pot. Cover and cook on LOW until the vegetables are tender and the flavors have blended, 6 to 8 hours. In a measuring cup, mix the water and cornstarch, and pour the mixture into the stew. Mix well and heat until the liquid has thickened. Garnish with the parsley.

PER SERVING: About 234 calories, 3 g fat (11% of calories), 0.8 g saturated fat, 18 mg cholesterol, 629 mg sodium, 6.2 g dietary fiber.

COOK'S NOTE: Butternut squash is a hard vegetable with a hard rind. For easiest cutting, use a sharp, sturdy French chef's knife and work on a firm work surface.

Veal and Vegetable Stew with Merlot

2 teaspoons olive oil

1 pound (455 g) lean veal cubes

¼ teaspoon freshly ground black pepper

1 teaspoon dried oregano

¾ cup (180 ml) fat-free beef broth

½ cup (120 ml) Merlot

4 turnips, cut into ½-inch (13 mm) cubes

12 ounces (340 g) baby carrots

1 onion, thinly sliced

Look to turnips for assertive flavor in this earthy dish. It's easy to throw together and sure to satisfy the heartiest of appetites.

MAKES 4 SERVINGS   **MEDIUM CROCKERY POT**

Heat the oil in a large nonstick skillet over medium heat. Add the veal and season with the pepper and oregano. Sauté, stirring, until lightly browned, 7 to 10 minutes.

Combine veal, broth, wine, turnips, carrots, and onions in the crockery pot. Cover and cook on LOW or HIGH until the veal is cooked through and tender, and the vegetables are tender, 6 to 8 hours on LOW or 4 to 5 hours on HIGH.

PER SERVING: 283 calories, 6.9 g fat, 160 mg sodium, 5 g dietary fiber.

QUICK TIP: Any other dry red wine can be substituted for the Merlot.

Peasant Goulash

2 teaspoons olive oil

1 pound (455 g) beef bottom round roast, cut into ½-inch (13 mm) cubes

4 onions, cut into thin wedges

3 ounces (75 g) button mushroom caps

1 cup (240 ml) fat-free beef broth

1 can (14 ounces, 400 g) stewed tomatoes

2 cloves garlic, crushed

1 teaspoon cocoa

2 tablespoons paprika

½ teaspoon marjoram

¼ teaspoon freshly ground black pepper

1 teaspoon browning and seasoning sauce

8 ounces (228 g) wide noodles

The flavor in this goulash is rich, deep, and complex — thanks to cocoa and tons of paprika. Serve over noodles, as suggested in the recipe, or over split baked potatoes.

MAKES 6 SERVINGS   **MEDIUM CROCKERY POT**

Heat the oil in a large nonstick skillet over medium-high heat. Add the beef, onions, and mushrooms, and sauté, stirring occasionally, until beef is lightly browned and the onions are translucent, 6 to 8 minutes.

Remove the beef mixture to the crockery pot. Pour the broth into the same skillet. Cook over medium heat, stirring and scraping constantly, for 2 minutes to deglaze the skillet. Pour into the beef mixture. Stir in the tomatoes, garlic, cocoa, paprika, marjoram, and pepper. Cover and cook on LOW or HIGH until the beef is are very tender, 6 to 8 hours on LOW or 4 to 6 hours on HIGH. Stir in the browning sauce.

Cook the noodles according to package directions. Drain well and divide among 6 plates. Top with the beef mixture.

PER SERVING: 338 calories, 5.9 g fat, 230 mg sodium, 4.2 g dietary fiber.

Red and White Vegetable Stew with Pork

1 teaspoon olive oil

1 boneless pork chop, trimmed of fat and cut into ½-inch (13 mm) cubes (about 6 ounces, 170 g)

1 onion, chopped

4 cloves garlic, minced

1 teaspoon cumin seeds

¼ teaspoon freshly ground black pepper

1 large turnip, chopped

1 large russet potato, peeled and cubed

2 cups (456 g) rinsed and drained canned red kidney beans

1 can (14 ounces, 420 ml) fat-free chicken broth

1 can (8 ounces, 228 g) no-salt-added tomato sauce

½ teaspoon fennel seeds

Simply soul-warming, this easy-to-prepare stew will reward you with complex flavors and heady aromas.

MAKES 4 SERVINGS   **MEDIUM CROCKERY POT**

Heat the oil in a nonstick skillet over medium-high heat. Add the pork, onion, garlic, cumin seeds, and pepper, and sauté, stirring, until the pork is lightly browned and the onion is translucent.

Combine the pork mixture, turnips, potatoes, beans, broth, tomato sauce, and fennel seeds in the crockery pot. Cover and cook on LOW until the pork is cooked through, the potato is tender, and the flavors are blended, 6 to 8 hours.

PER SERVING: 294 calories, 4.8 g fat, 155 mg sodium, 10 g dietary fiber.

QUICK TIP: Approximately 2 cups of beans are in a 15-ounce can.

Turkey, Carrot and Apple Stew

Olive-oil nonstick spray

1¼ pounds (568 g) boneless, skinless
   turkey breast slices, cut into strips

2 onions, cut into wedges

1 can (14 ounce, 420 ml) fat-free
   chicken broth

1 rib celery, sliced ¼ inch (6 mm) thick

½ cup (80 g) raisins

6 carrots, sliced ½ inch (13 mm) thick

1 teaspoon brown sugar

½ teaspoon curry powder

⅛ teaspoon ground turmeric

1½ cups (227 g) chopped
   McIntosh apples

2 tablespoons cornstarch

3 tablespoons cold water

1 teaspoon Louisiana hot sauce, or
   to taste

At the end of a busy day, beat the clock with this sensational dish that mixes sweet (apples and raisins) with spicy (curry and hot pepper sauce).

MAKES 4 SERVINGS   **MEDIUM CROCKERY POT**

Coat a nonstick skillet with the spray and heat it over medium-high heat. Add the turkey and onions, and cook, stirring, until browned, 4 to 6 minutes.

Combine the turkey mixture, broth, celery, raisins, carrots, brown sugar, curry powder, and turmeric in the crockery pot. Cover and cook on LOW until the turkey is cooked through and tender, 6 to 8 hours.

Stir in the apples. Cover the crockery pot, and cook for 1 to 2 minutes to soften the apples.

In a small cup, whisk together the cold water and cornstarch. Stir into the turkey mixture, and cook until the sauce has thickened, 1 to 5 minutes.

PER SERVING: 574 calories, 1.6 g fat (2% of calories), 0.4 g saturated fat, 118 mg cholesterol, 222 mg sodium, 6.2 g dietary fiber.

QUICK TIP: When McIntosh apples aren't in season, use almost any other popular apple: Cortland, Empire, Golden Delicious, Granny Smith, Rome Beauty, Winesap.

Bratwurst Simmered in Beer

½ pound (226 g) bratwurst, sliced
   ½ inch (13 mm) thick

4 medium potatoes, peeled and sliced
   ½ inch (13 mm) thick

3 parsnips, peeled and cut into
   2-inch (5 cm) cubes

3 medium onions, quartered

1 bottle (12 ounces, 300 ml)
   Oktoberfest-style beer

This is an absolutely delicious "wurst" case cooking event.

MAKES 4 SERVINGS   **LARGE CROCKERY POT**

Brown the bratwurst in a nonstick skillet over medium-high heat. Transfer it to the crockery pot.

In the same skillet, brown the potatoes, parsnips, and onions. Transfer the vegetables to the crockery pot. Pour in the beer. Cover and cook on LOW until the meat is done and the vegetables are tender, 6 to 8 hours.

PER SERVING: About 261 calories, 10 g fat (34% of calories), 3.6 g saturated fat, 23 mg cholesterol, 225 mg sodium, 4.6 g dietary fiber.

COOK'S NOTE: Fully cooked sausage needs less cooking time.

TURKEY, CARROT AND APPLE STEW

Super Soups

Cabbage Soup with Walnuts

4 slices bacon

2 cans (14 ounces, 420 ml, each) fat-free chicken broth

4 cups coarsely chopped green cabbage

1 large onion, chopped

1 carrot, thinly sliced

¼ teaspoon freshly ground black pepper

¼ teaspoon celery seeds

1 cup (120 g) nonfat sour cream

2 tablespoons chopped walnuts, toasted

2 tablespoons grated Provolone cheese

Dare to be different—by serving this smartly simple soup. It has an exceptional yet unique flavor that comes from a combination of bacon, toasted walnuts, and Provolone cheese.

MAKES 4 SERVINGS   **MEDIUM CROCKERY POT**

In a skillet, cook the bacon over medium heat until crisp. Remove to a plate lined with paper towels. Crumble.

Combine the broth, cabbage , onions, carrots, pepper, celery seeds, and bacon in the crockery pot. Cover and cook on LOW or HIGH until the carrots are tender, 5 to 6 hours on LOW or 3 to 4 hours on HIGH.

Stir in the sour cream and walnuts. Garnish each serving with the cheese.

PER SERVING: 186 calories, 4.6 g fat, 317 mg sodium, 3.4 g dietary fiber.

QUICK TIP: To toast the walnuts, place them in a small nonstick skillet over low heat. Cook, stirring frequently, until slightly browned and fragrant.

Lime Chicken Rice Soup

2 cans (14 ounces, 420 ml, each) fat-free chicken broth

1 rib celery, sliced diagonally into ½-inch (13 mm) pieces

2 carrots, sliced ½ inch (13 mm) thick

1 onion, chopped

1 bay leaf

½ pound (228 g) boneless, skinless chicken breast, cut into ½-inch (13 mm) pieces

1 cup (200 g) long-grain rice

Juice of 1 lime

1 teaspoon grated lime peel

½ teaspoon freshly ground black pepper

1 teaspoon snipped fresh lemon thyme or ¼ teaspoon dried

Anytime is a good time to enjoy chicken soup—the home-style favorite that's said to perk you up when you're feeling down with a cold or the flu. In this easy version, you'll find a new twist—a twist of lime, to be specific.

MAKES 4 SERVINGS   **MEDIUM CROCKERY POT**

Combine the broth, celery, carrots, onion, bay leaf, and chicken in the crockery pot. Cover and cook on LOW just until the chicken is almost cooked through, 4 to 5 hours on LOW. Stir in the rice, cover and cook on LOW until the rice is tender, 1½ to 3 hours.

Discard the bay leaf. Stir in the lime juice and peel, black pepper, and thyme. Cover and cook for 5 minutes.

PER SERVING: 207 calories, 2.3 g fat (10% of calories), 1 g saturated fat, 48 mg cholesterol, 205 mg sodium, 2.3 g dietary fiber.

Cream of Tomato Soup

1 can (28 ounces, 855 g) plum tomatoes,
    cut up

1 can (14 ounces) fat-free beef broth

1 medium onion, finely chopped

1 teaspoon butter

1 teaspoon Louisiana hot sauce

½ teaspoon dried thyme leaves

1 teaspoon sugar

½ cup (100 g) rice

2 teaspoons red wine vinegar

¼ teaspoon black pepper

½ cup (120 ml) half-and-half
    (or light cream)

Move over canned soup . . . this freshly made one rates tasters' choice. Its preparation is almost as simple as the store-bought version–honest.

MAKES 4 SERVINGS   **MEDIUM CROCKERY POT**

Combine the tomatoes, broth, onions, butter, hot sauce, thyme, sugar, rice, vinegar, and pepper in the crockery pot. Cover and cook on HIGH for 3½ to 5 hours. Using a hand-held blender, puree the soup. Stir in the half-and-half.

PER SERVING: About 202 calories, 5.1 g fat (23% of calories), 2.9 g saturated fat, 14 mg cholesterol, 384 mg sodium, 2.5 g dietary fiber.

COOK'S NOTE: Fresh out of half-and-half? Substitute canned evaporated skim milk; the taste and texture will be just fine.

Cream of Scallop Soup

1 pound (455 g) potatoes, peeled and
    cut into ½-inch (13 mm) cubes

¼ cup (60 ml) vegetable broth

2½ cups (600 ml) water

1 tablespoon white wine vinegar

1 medium onion, chopped

1 carrot, finely shredded

¼ teaspoon dried thyme leaves

¼ teaspoon garlic powder

1 egg yolk, lightly beaten

1 cup (240 ml) skim milk

½ pound (228 g) bay scallops or
    sea scallops

2 cups (170 g) shredded reduced-fat
    Cheddar cheese

Freshly ground black pepper,
    for garnish

Sprigs of parsley, for garnish

A soup so rich and flavorful you'd think it was laden with butter and cream—but it's not. For a complete meal, pair the soup with a crisp salad.

MAKES 8 SERVINGS   **MEDIUM CROCKERY POT**

Combine the potatoes, broth, water, vinegar, onions, carrots, thyme, and garlic in the crockery pot. Cover and cook on HIGH until the vegetables are tender, 4 to 6 hours (on LOW, 7 to 9 hours). Using a hand-held blender, puree the vegetables.

Add the scallops and cook, covered, for 10 minutes. Stir in the milk and egg yolk. Cook until the soup is hot throughout and the scallops are done, 30 to 60 minutes.

Mix in the cheese and cook until it's melted, about 5 minutes. Divide the soup among 8 bowls, and garnish each serving with the pepper and parsley.

PER SERVING: About 185 calories, 6 g fat (30% of calories), 3.3 g saturated fat, 59 mg cholesterol, 229 mg sodium, 1.4 g dietary fiber.

COOK'S NOTE: If you use sea scallops, halve small ones and quarter large ones.

Lima Bean and Macaroni Soup

½ cup (120 ml) water

2 cans (14 ounces, 420 ml, each)
    fat-free chicken broth

1 cup (150 g) frozen baby lima beans,
    thawed

¼ pound (114 g) lean ham, cut into
    ¼-inch (6 mm) cubes

2 onions, chopped

1 rib celery, chopped

4 plum tomatoes, peeled and chopped

4 cloves garlic, chopped

½ cup macaroni

1 cup (80 g) torn fresh mustard greens

1 teaspoon marjoram

⅛ teaspoon freshly ground
    black pepper

This home-style dish is a meal in itself. It's lean; it's easy; it's delicious.

MAKES 6 SERVINGS   **MEDIUM CROCKERY POT**

Combine the water, broth, beans, ham, onions, celery, tomatoes, and garlic in the crockery pot. Cover and cook on LOW or HIGH until the flavors are blended, 5 to 6 hours on LOW or 3 to 4 hours on HIGH.

Meanwhile, cook the pasta according to package directions and drain well. Stir the greens, macaroni, marjoram, and pepper into the bean mixture. Cover and cook on LOW or HIGH until the greens are wilted, 10 to 20 minutes on LOW or 5 to 15 minutes on HIGH.

PER SERVING: 152 calories, 1.1 g fat (6% of calories), 0.2 g saturated fat, 3.1 mg cholesterol, 182 mg sodium, 4.7 g dietary fiber.

QUICK TIP: Add marjoram, a mild herb with an oreganolike flavor, to foods near the end of cooking; otherwise, its delicate essence may dissipate.

Curried Crookneck Squash Soup with Ginger

1 medium crookneck squash
    (2½ pounds, 1.14 kg), peeled and
    cut into 1-inch (2.5 cm) cubes (1
    medium yellow summer squash
    can substitute)

1 medium onion, chopped

1 carrot, coarsely shredded

3 cups (720 ml) fat-free chicken broth

2 teaspoons gingerroot, finely chopped

1 teaspoon curry powder

½ cup (120 ml) half-and-half

Paprika, for garnish

Ginger and curry transform mild crookneck squash into a special taste-bud pleaser. The soup's visually appealing and a terrific source of vitamin A, as well.

MAKES 8 SERVINGS   **MEDIUM CROCKERY POT**

Combine the squash, onions, carrots, and broth in the crockery pot. Stir in the gingerroot and curry powder. Cover and cook on LOW until the squash is tender, 7 to 9 hours (on HIGH, 4 to 6 hours).

Using a hand-held blender, puree the vegetables. Stir in the half-and-half. Divide the soup among 8 bowls. Swirl in the paprika.

PER SERVING: About 93 calories, 2.1 g fat (19% of calories), 1.2 g saturated fat, 5.6 mg cholesterol, 141 mg sodium, 0.6 g dietary fiber.

COOK'S NOTES: Popular butternut or acorn squash can replace the crookneck. Don't own a hand-held blender? Mash the vegetables. Or let the soup cool slightly and puree it in batches in a food processor.

Hearty Corn Chowder with Peas

2 teaspoons olive oil

2 ounces (57 g) Italian sausage, chopped into ½-inch (13 mm) cubes

1 large onion, chopped

4 cloves garlic, minced

1 can (14 ounces, 420 ml) low-sodium vegetable broth

2 russet potatoes, peeled and cut into ½-inch (13 mm) cubes

1 can (15 ounces, 426 g) cream-style corn

1 cup (150 g) frozen corn, thawed

½ cup (75 g) frozen peas, thawed

1 teaspoon Crystal brand Louisiana-style hot sauce

Thick, flavorful chowders like this one are always a big hit with my family. This potato–corn version gets a spicy kick from Italian sausage and hot pepper sauce.

MAKES 4 SERVINGS   **MEDIUM CROCKERY POT**

Heat the oil in a skillet over medium-high heat. Add the sausage, onions, and garlic, and. sauté, stirring, until the sausage is lightly brown and the onions are translucent, 5 to 8 minutes.

Combine the sausage mixture, broth, and potatoes in the crockery pot. Cover and cook on LOW or HIGH until the potatoes are very tender, 5 to 6 hours on LOW or 3 to 4 hours on HIGH. Using the back of a spoon, coarsely mash the potatoes. Stir in the cream-style corn and the corn. Cover, turn the crockery pot to HIGH, and cook for 1 hour. Stir in the peas and cook until the mixture is hot and the peas are tender, about 10 minutes. Stir in the hot sauce.

PER SERVING: 266 calories, 6.4g fat, 188 mg sodium, 8.3 g dietary fiber.

QUICK TIP: The intensity of hot sauces varies from mild, such as the Crystal brand used in this recipe, to scorching, such as Tabasco sauce. If using a variety other than Crystal, add it by the drop and taste-test after each addition.

Ham and Black Bean Soup with Chilies

Nonstick spray

½ pound (228 g) lean ham, finely chopped

2 cans (14 ounces, 420 ml, each) fat-free beef broth

1 can (15 ounces, 426 g) black beans, rinsed and drained

2 medium onions, chopped

2 medium-hot chili peppers (such as jalapeño, serrano, or poblano), finely chopped

1 large sweet green pepper, chopped

2 carrots, coarsely shredded

1 bay leaf

½ teaspoon cumin seeds

Shredded carrots add a splash of color to this peppery soup.

MAKES 6 SERVINGS   **MEDIUM CROCKERY POT**

Coat a skillet with nonstick spray and warm it over medium-high heat. Brown the ham, about 5 minutes. Transfer it to the crockery pot.

Stir in the broth, beans, onions, chilies, sweet peppers, carrots, bay leaf, and cumin. Cover and cook on LOW for 6 to 8 hours or on HIGH for 4 to 6 hours. Discard the bay leaf.

PER SERVING: About 182 calories, 2.6 g fat (13% of calories), 0.8 g saturated fat, 21 mg cholesterol, 555 mg sodium, 4.2 g dietary fiber.

COOK'S NOTE: If you prefer a less nippy soup, use only 1 medium-hot chili or substitute a mild variety, such as Anaheim.

HEARTY CORN CHOWDER WITH PEAS

Cream of Portobello Mushroom–Barley Soup

6 ounces (170 g) portobello
    mushrooms, chopped into
    ½-inch (13 mm) cubes

1 medium onion, minced

1 teaspoon tub-style margarine

2 cans (14 ounces, 420 ml, each)
    fat-free beef broth

¼ cup (60 ml) dry sherry

¼ cup barley

¼ teaspoon dried sage

⅛ teaspoon garlic powder

⅛ teaspoon white pepper

1 can (12 ounces, 340 ml)) evaporated
    skim milk

Fresh snipped parsley, for garnish

This light soup is deliciously flavored with fresh, meaty mushrooms. Serve as a luncheon main course or a dinner first course.

MAKES 4 SERVINGS　　　　　　　　**MEDIUM CROCKERY POT**

Sauté the mushrooms and onions in the margarine in a nonstick skillet over medium-high heat, 4 to 5 minutes. Transfer the vegetables to the crockery pot. Stir in the broth, sherry, barley, sage, garlic, and pepper. Cover and cook on LOW until the barley is tender, 6 to 8 hours (on HIGH, 4 to 6 hours).

Stir in the milk, and cook until hot, 15 to 30 minutes. Divide the soup among 4 bowls, and garnish each serving with the parsley.

PER SERVING: About 164 calories, 1.2 g fat (6% of calories), 0.3 g saturated fat, 3.1 mg cholesterol, 252 mg sodium, 2.8 g dietary fiber.

COOK'S NOTE: Eight ounces (227 g) of white button mushrooms, which are less meaty in texture and flavor, can replace the portobellos.

Hearty Kielbasa Soup

¼ pound (114 g) light kielbasa, cut in
    half lengthwise and thinly sliced

1 medium onion, chopped

4 cloves garlic, minced

1 sweet green pepper, chopped

1 celery stalk, thinly sliced

2 cans (14 ounces, 420 ml, each)
    fat-free chicken broth

1 can (15 ounces, 426 g) stewed
    tomatoes

1 cup (228 g) canned pinto beans,
    rinsed and drained

1 medium carrot, coarsely shredded

1 small zucchini, thinly sliced

¼ cup (20 g) snipped fresh parsley or
    1 tablespoon dried

¼ teaspoon crushed red pepper flakes

¼ teaspoon freshly ground
    black pepper

Psyched for the spicy flavor of sausage? It's here in a wonderfully zesty dish that's a snap to make. Serve with sourdough or Russian rye bread.

MAKES 8 SERVINGS　　　　　　　　**LARGE CROCKERY POT**

Brown the kielbasa in a nonstick skillet over medium-high heat, about 5 minutes. Add the onions, garlic, green pepper, and celery. Sauté until the onions are lightly browned, 1 to 3 minutes.

Transfer the kielbasa mixture to the crockery pot. Add the broth, tomatoes, beans, carrots, zucchini, parsley, red and black peppers. Cover and cook on LOW for 7 to 9 hours or on HIGH for 4 to 6 hours.

PER SERVING: About 185 calories, 3.1 g fat (14% of calories), 0.1 g saturated fat, 0 mg cholesterol, 493 mg sodium, 6.1 g dietary fiber.

COOK'S NOTE: This soup is still delicious after a day or two in the refrigerator. Heat on the stove top or in the microwave until hot and bubbly.

Italian-Style Tomato Soup

2 teaspoons olive oil

1 onion, finely chopped

1 carrot, finely chopped

1 celery rib, finely chopped

4 cloves garlic, thinly sliced

1 can (28 ounces, 800 g) crushed
    tomatoes

1 can (14 ounces, 420 ml) fat-free
    beef broth

1 tablespoon red wine vinegar

1 can (19 ounces, 540 g) garbanzo beans
    (chick peas), rinsed, drained,
    and mashed

1 tablespoon oregano

¼ teaspoon freshly ground black pepper

6 fresh basil leaves, snipped

This singular soup gets its rich texture from pureed garbanzo beans and its enticing hint of licorice from fresh basil.

MAKES 6 SERVINGS   **LARGE CROCKERY POT**

Heat the oil in a nonstick skillet over medium-high heat. Add the onion, carrot, celery, and garlic, and sauté, stirring, until the onion is lightly browned.

Combine the tomatoes, broth, vinegar, beans, onion mixture, oregano, and pepper in the crockery pot. Cover and cook on LOW or HIGH until the vegetables are tender and the flavors are blended, 5 to 6 hours on LOW or 3 to 4 hours on HIGH. Stir in the basil.

PER SERVING: 162 calories, 2.9 g fat, 376 mg sodium, 6.7 g dietary fiber.

QUICK TIP: To snip the basil quickly, stack the leaves and cut them all at once.

Chorizo–Tortilla Soup

1 teaspoon olive oil

2 onions, finely chopped

4 cloves garlic, minced

1 green bell pepper, finely chopped

3 ounces (85 g) cooked chorizo,
    thinly sliced

3 cups (600 g) crushed tomatoes

1 can (14½ ounces, 435 ml) fat-free
    chicken broth

1 dried cayenne pepper, seeded and
    minced, or 1 teaspoon crushed red
    pepper flakes

1 teaspoon chopped fresh cilantro

6 baked tortilla chips, broken

¾ cup (60 g) shredded
    cheddar cheese

Crunchy chips top this zesty, Mexican-style soup. Cayenne pepper and chorizo, a spicy sausage, add the zing while cheddar cheese soothes the bite.

MAKES 4 SERVINGS   **MEDIUM CROCKERY POT**

Heat the oil in a large nonstick skillet over medium-high heat. Add the onions, garlic, bell pepper, and chorizo and sauté, stirring, just until the onions turn golden.

Combine the onion mixture, tomatoes, broth, and cayenne pepper or pepper flakes in the crockery pot. Cover and cook on LOW or HIGH until the flavors are blended, 5 to 6 hours on LOW or 3 to 4 hours on HIGH. Stir in the cilantro.

Divide the soup among 4 bowls, and top each serving with the tortilla chips and cheese.

PER SERVING: 240 calories, 7.2 g fat, 910 mg sodium, 3.2 g dietary fiber.

QUICK TIP: Toasted flour tortillas or crisp, broken taco shells can replace the tortilla chips.

ONION-LEEK SOUP

Onion-Leek Soup

2 leeks, white part only, thinly sliced

3 medium onions, thinly sliced and separated into rings

1 teaspoon olive oil

4 cloves garlic, pressed

1 cup (240 ml) vegetable broth

3 cups (720 ml) water

1½ tablespoons white wine vinegar

2 bay leaves

4 fresh sage leaves

⅛ teaspoon white pepper

¼ cup (20 g) shredded reduced-fat Swiss cheese

2 cups garlic croutons

For a healthful indulgence in French onion soup, be sure to try this slow-simmered version with a Swiss twist.

MAKES 4 SERVINGS   **LARGE CROCKERY POT**

Sauté the leeks and onions in the oil in a nonstick skillet over medium-high heat until lightly browned. Transfer the vegetables to the crockery pot. Stir in the garlic, broth, water, vinegar, bay leaves, sage, and white pepper. Cover and cook on LOW for 6 to 8 hours or on HIGH for 4 to 6 hours. Discard the bay leaves. Divide the soup among 4 bowls, and top each serving with a quarter of the cheese and croutons.

PER SERVING: About 198 calories, 3.9 g fat (17% of calories), 1.2 g saturated fat, 4.5 mg cholesterol, 199 mg sodium, 3.1 g dietary fiber.

COOK'S NOTE: To make 2 cups **garlic croutons,** cut approximately 4 slices of firm bread into fl-inch cubes. Place the cubes on a baking sheet or a perforated pizza pan. Mist the cubes with nonstick spray, and sprinkle them with garlic powder. Broil them until they're golden, about 5 minutes. Shake or stir the cubes to expose the uncooked sides; broil them until golden, about 3 minutes.

Lamb–Vegetable Soup

Olive-oil cooking spray

¾ pound (340 g) lean lamb, cut into ¾-inch (20 mm) cubes

1 can (14 ounces, 400 g) stewed tomatoes

1 cup cooked barley

2½ cups (600 ml) fat-free beef broth

6 cloves garlic, minced

2 onions, chopped

4 carrots, sliced

2 potatoes, cut into ½-inch (13 mm) cubes

2 teaspoons dried sage

1 cup (80 g) torn kale

½ teaspoon freshly ground black pepper

Kale, a crisp, vitamin-A-packed green that's plentiful in the fall, perks up this casual soup.

MAKES 4 SERVINGS   **MEDIUM CROCKERY POT**

Coat a nonstick skillet with the cooking spray and heat over medium-high heat. Add the lamb, and cook, stirring occasionally, until browned, 4 to 5 minutes. Remove to the crockery pot. Add the tomatoes, barley, garlic, onion, carrots, potatoes, and sage. Cover and cook on LOW until the lamb is cooked through and is tender, 6 to 8 hours.

Stir in the kale and pepper. Cover and cook until the kale is wilted, 5 to 10 minutes.

PER SERVING: 429 calories, 6.9 g fat (14% of calories), 2.2 g saturated fat, 74 mg cholesterol, 439 mg sodium, 10.6 g dietary fiber.

QUICK TIP: To remove garlic's tenacious skin, wrap the clove in a rubber jar-gripper and, applying a little pressure, roll the clove on the countertop. Zap, the garlic's skinless!

Ukrainian-Style Borscht

2 cans (14 ounces, 420 ml, each)
    fat-free beef broth

¾ pound (340 g) eye of round steak, cut
    into ½-inch (13 mm) cubes

1 cup (228 g) rinsed and drained
    canned small white beans

1 onion, cut into thin wedges

4 beets, peeled and cut into
    ½-inch (13 mm) cubes

1 tablespoon red wine vinegar

2 cups coarsely sliced cabbage

¼ teaspoon freshly ground
    black pepper

¼ cup (10 g) snipped fresh dill

Nonfat sour cream, garnish

Just 10 fresh ingredients—not the usual 20 to 30—make up this easy but traditional-tasting beet soup.

MAKES 4 SERVINGS　　　　**MEDIUM CROCKERY POT**

Combine the broth, beef, beans, and onion in the crockery pot. Cover and cook on LOW for 6 to 7 hours. Stir in the onion, beets, and vinegar. Cover and cook on LOW until the beef and beets are tender, 1 to 2 hours.

Stir in the cabbage, pepper and dill. Cover and cook on LOW until the cabbage is tender, 10 to 15 minutes.

Divide the soup among 4 bowls; garnish each serving with a tablespoon of the sour cream.

PER SERVING: 317 calories, 4.6 g fat (13% of calories), 1.6 g saturated fat, 59 mg cholesterol, 268 mg sodium, 4.6 g dietary fiber.

QUICK TIPS: To use canned beets instead of the fresh varity, add the beets along with the cabbage and dill. And if you can't find any fresh dill, use 2 tablespoons dill weed instead.

Zucchini–Chicken Soup with Cheddar

2 cans (14 ounces, 420 ml, each)
    fat-free chicken broth

2 large russet potatoes, peeled
    and chopped

1 cup (240 ml) water

1 zucchini, shredded

½ pound cooked chicken breast, cut
    into bite-size pieces

4 cloves garlic, crushed

½ teaspoon dried marjoram leaves

Pinch of white pepper

1 cup (85 g) shredded reduced-fat sharp
    cheddar cheese

Oyster crackers (optional)

When the markets — or your garden — overflow with zucchini and summer squash, here's a deliciously easy way to use some of nature's bounty. Cheddar cheese gives the soup an incomparable richness; garlic and marjoram provide just the right seasoning.

MAKES 4 SERVINGS　　　　**MEDIUM CROCKERY POT**

Combine the broth, potatoes, water, zucchini, chicken, garlic, marjoram, and white pepper in the crockery pot. Cover and cook on LOW or HIGH until the potatoes are very tender, 5 to 6 hours on LOW or 3 to 4 hours on HIGH.

Stir in the cheese. Using a hand-held immersion blender, partially puree the mixture. Serve immediately with the crackers, if using.

PER SERVING: 296 calories, 5.2 g fat, 242 mg sodium, 2.7 g dietary fiber.

QUICK TIP: About 2 teaspoons crushed garlic from a jar equals 4 garlic cloves.

Carrot–Fava Bean Soup with Roasted Peppers

2 cans (14 ounces, 420 ml, each)
   fat-free chicken broth

2 cups (460 g) rinsed and drained
   canned fava beans

2 potatoes, peeled and cubed

2 carrots, shredded

¼ cup chopped roasted red peppers

¼ teaspoon freshly ground
   black pepper

4 cloves garlic, crushed

This toss-everything-together soup goes together in about 5 minutes, and it cooks all day—so it's perfect for those busy nights when you're feeling too frazzled to fuss over the stove. Fava beans, which have a delightful buttery texture, replace the usual soup beans — red kidney, white, or cannellini.

MAKES 4 SERVINGS   **MEDIUM CROCKERY POT**

Combine the broth, fava beans, potatoes, carrots, red peppers, black pepper, and garlic in the crockery pot. Cover and cook on LOW or HIGH until the potatoes are tender and the flavors are blended, 5 to 6 hours on LOW or 3 to 4 hours on HIGH.

PER SERVING: 240 calories, 0.6 g fat, 362 mg sodium, 7.9 g dietary fiber.

QUICK TIP: In this recipe, use either roasted red peppers from a jar, or roast your own. For the freshly roasted version, grill or broil a red bell pepper until tender and slightly charred on all sides, 10 to 12 minutes, turning with tongs as needed. Transfer to a glass baking dish with a lid. Close and let steam for 10 minutes. Rub off and discard the charred skin. Quarter and discard the seeds. Chop.

Potato and Leek Soup with Ham

Nonstick spray

6 ounces (170 g) ham, cut into
   ¼-inch cubes

2 large leeks, white parts only,
   thinly sliced

4 large potatoes, peeled and
   finely shredded

2 cans (14 ounces, 420 ml, each)
   fat-free chicken broth

⅛ teaspoon black pepper

1 cup (240 ml) skim milk

8 ounces (228 g) nonfat ricotta cheese

Snipped fresh parsley

A little ham adds lots of texture and flavor to this comforting soup. For some crunch, serve with melba toast.

MAKES 8 SERVINGS   **MEDIUM CROCKERY POT**

Coat a skillet with nonstick spray and warm it over medium-high heat. Add the ham, and cook it until lightly browned, about 5 minutes. Add the leeks, and cook until they're translucent, 3 to 4 minutes. Transfer the ham and leeks to the crockery pot.

Stir in the potatoes, broth, and pepper. Cover and cook on LOW until the potatoes are tender, 6 to 8 hours (on HIGH, 4 to 6 hours). Stir well to break up the potatoes.

Stir in the milk and cheese, and cook until the soup is hot, 5 to 15 minutes. Divide the soup among 8 bowls, and garnish each serving with the parsley.

PER SERVING: About 151 calories, 1.5 g (9% of calories), 0.5 g saturated fat, 12 mg cholesterol, 476 mg sodium, 1.7 g dietary fiber.

COOK'S NOTES: Shredding the potatoes before cooking eliminates the need for mashing them afterward. Though best when served fresh, this soup will keep for a day in the refrigerator.

FRESH MANHATTAN CLAM CHOWDER

Fresh Manhattan Clam Chowder

3 slices bacon

2 celery stalks, finely chopped

3 medium onions, finely chopped

4 small potatoes, diced

2 carrots, diced

½ teaspoon dried thyme leaves

¼ teaspoon black pepper

⅛ teaspoon Louisiana hot sauce,
   or to taste

1 pint minced clams or 2 cans
   (6½ ounces, 186 g, each)

1 can (28 ounces, 800 g) stewed
   tomatoes, cut up

½ cups (40 g) snipped fresh parsley

Never shucked a clam? No problem. Succulent minced clams are readily available in the fish section of most large supermarkets.

MAKES 8 SERVINGS   **LARGE CROCKERY POT**

Cook the bacon in a skillet over medium-high heat until it's crisp, about 5 minutes. Drain the bacon on paper towels. Crumble the bacon into the crockery pot. Discard the drippings, leaving about 1 teaspoon in the skillet. Sauté the celery and onions in the bacon drippings in the same skillet until golden, 3 to 4 minutes. Transfer the onion mixture to the crockery pot. Stir in the potatoes, carrots, thyme, pepper, and hot sauce.

Drain the liquid from the clams into a pint measuring cup (480 ml). Add enough water to it to make 2 cups (480ml) of liquid. Add the clam liquid–water mixture (not the clams) to the crockery pot. Stir in the tomatoes. Cover and cook on LOW for 6 to 8 hours or on HIGH for 4 to 6 hours. During the last hour of cooking, stir in the minced clams. Cover and cook for 1 hour. Stir in the parsley and cook for 15 minutes.

PER SERVING: About 145 calories, 2.2 g fat (13% of calories), 0.5 g saturated fat, 21 mg cholesterol, 253 mg sodium, 3.3 g dietary fiber.

COOK'S NOTES: Fresh minced clams shouldn't smell fishy. If they do, return them to the store for a truly fresh batch.

This chowder will keep for up to 3 days in the refrigerator.

Sweet Sausage and White Bean Soup

2 ounces (57 g) cooked sweet Italian
   sausage, thinly sliced

1 can (14½ ounces, 414 g) stewed sliced
   tomatoes

1 can (14½ ounces, 540 ml) fat-free beef
   broth

2 cups (450 g) rinsed and drained
   canned cannellini beans

1 large carrot, thinly sliced

1 potato, finely chopped

3 sprigs thyme

1 tablespoon chili sauce

So simple. So tasty. So easy to make that you can whip up this rustic soup for a fuss-free weeknight dinner. Serve with a crusty bread for sopping up the flavorful broth.

MAKES 4 SERVINGS   **MEDIUM CROCKERY POT**

Combine the sausage, tomatoes, broth, beans, carrots, potatoes, thyme, and chili sauce in the crockery pot. Cover and cook on LOW or HIGH until the carrot and potato are tender, 5 to 6 hours on LOW or 3 to 4 hours on HIGH. Discard the thyme sprigs.

PER SERVING: 225 calories, 1.1 g fat, 381 mg sodium, 8.6 g dietary fiber.

Beef Noodle Soup Bolognese

1 teaspoon butter

1 large onion, chopped

2 ounces (57 g) prosciutto, chopped

1 teaspoon olive oil

¾ pound ground beef sirloin

1 cup (114 g) white mushrooms, chopped

4 cups (960 ml) fat-free beef broth

1 can (15 ounces, 426 g) diced tomatoes

2 teaspoons no-salt-added tomato paste

½ teaspoon freshly ground black pepper

4 ounces (114 g) wide egg noodles

1 cup garlic croutons

Ladle up matchless gourmet flavor with this captivating soup. Traditional Bolognese, named after the rich culinary style of Bologna, Italy, refers to a flavorful meat and vegetable sauce that's often served over pasta.

MAKES 4 SERVINGS   **MEDIUM CROCKERY POT**

Melt the butter in a skillet. Add the onions, prosciutto, and oil, and cook until the onions are golden, about 5 minutes. Add the beef and the mushrooms, and cook, stirring, until the beef is browned and crumbly, about 8 minutes. Drain off excess liquid.

Combine in the broth, tomatoes, tomato paste, beef mixture in the crockery pot. Cover and cook on LOW or HIGH until the flavors are blended, 5 to 6 hours on LOW or 3 to 4 hours on HIGH.

Cook the noodles according to package directions. Drain well and stir into the broth mixture. Stir in the noodles. Divide among 4 bowls and top each serving with the croutons.

PER SERVING: 395 calories, 9.3 g fat, 3 g saturated fat, 67 mg cholesterol, 432 mg sodium, 3.6 g dietary fiber.

QUICK TIP: To make croutons, cut white or whole-grain bread into ¾-inch cubes. Arrange on a baking sheet and mist with cooking spray and sprinkle with powdered garlic. Broil until golden, about 3 minutes. Stir to expose the untoasted sides. Mist with cooking spray and broil another 2 to 3 minutes.

Turkey–Split Pea Soup

1 teaspoon olive oil

½ pound (228 g) turkey breast cutlets, cut into ¾-inch (20 mm) pieces

1 onion, chopped

2 cans (14 ounces, 420 g, each) fat-free chicken broth

1 cup (240 ml) water

½ cup dried split peas, rinsed and sorted

1 large potato, peeled and cut into ½-inch (13 mm) pieces

1 carrot, thinly sliced

½ teaspoon celery seeds

1 bay leaf

Pinch of white pepper

Here's a wonderful home-style soup that'll warm your soul. It takes but minutes to put together; dried split peas are hearty but need no soaking or precooking. I serve it often with a crisp green salad and chewy Russian rye bread.

MAKES 4 SERVINGS   **MEDIUM CROCKERY POT**

Heat the oil in a large skillet over medium-high heat. Add the turkey and onions, and sauté, stirring occasionally, until lightly browned, about 6 minutes.

Combine the turkey mixture, broth, water, split peas, potatoes, carrots, celery seeds, bay leaf, and white pepper in the crockery pot. Cover and cook on LOW until the turkey is cooked through and the vegetables are tender, 5 to 6 hours. Discard the bay leaf.

PER SERVING: 260 calories, 2.3 g fat, 230 mg sodium, 9.1 g dietary fiber.

QUICK TIP: If you can find fresh bay leaves, give them a try. They have far more flavor than the dried variety.

Salmon, Corn, and Red Pepper Chowder

3 cups (320 g) corn

3 medium sweet red peppers, coarsely chopped

2 medium red potatoes, cut into ½-inch (13 mm) cubes

1 medium onion, chopped

1 can (14 ounces, 420 g) vegetable broth

1 cup (240 ml) water

2 fresh chili peppers, minced

4 cloves garlic, minced

2 tablespoons white wine vinegar

1 tablespoon chili powder

1 teaspoon cumin seed

1 teaspoon dried oregano

½ pound (228 g) salmon steak, bones removed and cut into 1½-inch (4 cm) cubes

Celebrate fresh salmon season with this spicy chowder, which is a meal in itself. And by the way, the vitamin C's high, thanks to potatoes and sweet red peppers.

MAKES 6 SERVINGS   **LARGE CROCKERY POT**

Combine the corn, sweet peppers, potatoes, onions, vegetable broth, and water in the crockery pot. Stir in the chili peppers, garlic, vinegar, chili powder, cumin, and oregano. Carefully stir in the salmon. Cover and cook on LOW until the vegetables are tender and the salmon is cooked through, 6 to 8 hours.

PER SERVING: About 272 calories, 4.8 g fat (15% of calories), 0.9 g saturated fat, 22 mg cholesterol, 64 mg sodium, 2.4 g dietary fiber.

COOK'S NOTE: For a chowder with less chili fire, use only 1 fresh chili pepper and 1½ teaspoons of chili powder.

Two-Pepper and Black Bean Soup

2 cans (14 ounces, 420 g each) fat-free
   chicken broth

2 russet potatoes, peeled and cubed

1 onion, chopped

1 cup (228 g) rinsed and drained
   canned black beans

2 teaspoons pressed garlic

1 rib celery, thinly sliced

1 carrot, chopped

½ green bell pepper, chopped

1 mild chili pepper, seeded and
   thinly sliced

3 ounces (85 g) cooked sausage, diced

½ teaspoon thyme

¼ teaspoon freshly ground
   black pepper

½ cup (120 g) fat-free sour cream

Set your palate for an exhilarating experience. This soup is spicy hot and sensational. But you can tame the heat by taking a cue from experienced Mexican cooks: Add a dollop of sour cream to each serving. Of course, you can also turn up the heat by choosing a hot variety of chili pepper.

MAKES 6 SERVINGS **MEDIUM CROCKERY POT**

Combine the broth, potatoes, onion, beans, garlic, celery, carrots, bell pepper, chili pepper, sausage, thyme, and black pepper in the crockery pot. Cover and cook on LOW or HIGH until the potatoes are tender and the flavors are blended, 5 to 6 hours on LOW or 3 to 4 hours on HIGH.

Divide the soup among 6 bowls. Top each serving with 1½ tablespoons of the sour cream.

PER SERVING: 203 calories, 4.3 g fat, 279 mg sodium, 4.8 g dietary fiber.

QUICK TIP: Wear gloves when seeding and chopping chili peppers; the chemical responsible for their culinary heat can sting your fingers.

Creamy Parsnip-Carrot Soup

2 tablespoons rice

1 pound (455 g) carrots, peeled and cut
   into 1-inch (2.5 cm) cubes

1 pound parsnips, peeled and cut into
   1-inch (2.5 cm) cubes

2 cups (480 ml) vegetable broth

1 cup (240 ml) water

1 cup (240 ml) evaporated skim milk

¼ teaspoon black pepper

2 tablespoons ground walnuts

A wonderful warmer-upper that gets its mellow, sweet-nutty flavor from parsnips—once as popular as today's ubiquitous potato.

MAKES 4 SERVINGS **MEDIUM CROCKERY POT**

Combine the rice, carrots, parsnips, vegetable broth, and water in the crockery pot. Cover and cook on LOW until the vegetables are tender, about 5 hours (on HIGH about 3 hours).

Using a hand-held blender, puree the vegetables. Stir in the milk and pepper. Heat the soup until hot, 5 to 10 minutes. Divide the soup among 4 bowls, and sprinkle each serving with 1½ teaspoons of walnuts.

PER SERVING: About 256 calories, 2.9 g fat (10% of calories), 0.3 g saturated fat, 2.3 mg cholesterol, 168 mg sodium, 8.8 g dietary fiber.

COOK'S NOTE: Like their cousins the carrots, the sweetest parsnips are slender and about 8 inches long.

White Bean Soup du Jour

1 can (16 ounces, 455 g) great northern beans, rinsed and drained

1 medium onion, quartered

2 cloves garlic, pressed

1 carrot, shredded

1 stalk celery, finely chopped

1 teaspoon dried thyme leaves

1 can (14 ounces, 420 g) fat-free chicken broth

½ cup (120 ml) half-and-half

2 plum tomatoes, seeded and chopped

Snipped fresh parsley, for garnish

Garlic croutons for garnish
(see page 54)

Tomatoes, parsley, and croutons create a medley of colors and textures atop this smooth, sophisticated cream-and-bean soup.

MAKES 4 SERVINGS **MEDIUM CROCKERY POT**

Combine the beans, onions, garlic, carrots, celery, thyme, and broth in the crockery pot. Cover and cook on LOW for 6 to 8 hours or on HIGH for 3½ to 5 hours.

Using a hand-held blender or a food processor, puree the bean soup. Stir in the half-and-half. Divide the soup among 4 bowls; top each serving with the tomatoes. Garnish with the parsley and garlic croutons.

PER SERVING: About 240 calories, 4.1 g fat (15% of calories), 2.3 g saturated fat, 11 mg cholesterol, 190 mg sodium, 7.1 g dietary fiber.

COOK'S NOTE: To seed the tomatoes, cut them in half, and gently squeeze out the seeds and pulp.

Southwest Chicken and Corn Chowder

1 can (14 ounces, 420 ml) fat-free chicken broth

1 pound boneless, skinless chicken breast, cut into ¾-inch (20 mm) cubes

1 medium sweet red pepper, chopped

1 medium sweet green pepper, chopped

1 medium onion, chopped

2 cloves garlic, minced

2 cans (8 ounces, 228 g, each) low-sodium cream-style corn

2 medium potatoes, cut into ½-inch (13 mm) cubes

1 cup (150 g) frozen corn

1 teaspoon cumin seeds

1 dried cayenne pepper, minced

2 tablespoons cornstarch

½ cup (120 ml) evaporated skim milk

Lots of cream-style corn combines with chicken and potatoes for a pleasingly chunky chowder. Cumin and jalapeño pepper provide the distinctive southwest flavor. Olé!

MAKES 8 SERVINGS **MEDIUM CROCKERY POT**

Combine the broth, chicken, sweet peppers, onions, garlic, cream-style corn, potatoes, frozen corn, cumin, and cayenne in the crockery pot. Cover and cook on LOW until the chicken is tender and cooked through, 8 to 10 hours.

In a measuring cup, mix the cornstarch and milk until blended. Pour into the chicken soup and cook until it is slightly thickened.

PER SERVING: About 221 calories, 2.8 g fat (11% of calories), 0.7 g saturated fat, 49 mg cholesterol, 143 mg sodium, 2 g dietary fiber.

COOK'S NOTE: If cumin seeds and a dried cayenne pepper aren't on hand, use ½ teaspoon ground cumin and 1 teaspoon crushed red pepper flakes instead.

Old-World Minestrone with Shell Pasta

1 carrot, shredded

1 celery stalk, sliced

¼ cup (37 g) frozen peas

1 medium potato, cut into
  ½-inch (13 mm) cubes

⅔ cup sliced scallions

2 cans (14 ounces, 420 ml, each) fat-free
  chicken or vegetable broth

1 teaspoon Italian herb seasoning
  or marjoram

1 can (28 ounces, 800 g) Italian plum
  tomatoes, cut up

Pinch of cayenne pepper

1 tablespoon red wine vinegar

1 cup (80 g) chopped escarole

½ cup shell pasta

½ cup (40 g) snipped fresh parsley

Parmesan cheese (optional)

Get ready for some hearty and healthful eating; the servings of this classic Italian soup are very generous!

MAKES 4 SERVINGS   **LARGE CROCKERY POT**

Combine the carrots, celery, peas, potatoes, scallions, broth, seasoning, tomatoes, pepper, and vinegar in the crockery pot. Cover and cook on LOW for 6 to 8 hours or on HIGH for 4 to 5 hours.

During the last 20 minutes of cooking, stir in the escarole and pasta. Divide the soup among 4 bowls, and top each serving with the parsley and cheese, if you wish.

PER SERVING: About 148 calories, 0.9 g fat (5% of calories), 0.1 g saturated fat, 0 mg cholesterol, 640 mg sodium, 3.9 g dietary fiber.

COOK'S NOTE: This vegetable-packed soup is best when freshly made.

Creamy Potato Soup

2 cups (240 ml) water

4 packages low-sodium
  chicken bouillion

2 cups (450 g) rinsed and drained
  canned great northern beans

3 russet potatoes, peeled and
  ½-inch (13 mm) cubes

¼ teaspoon celery seeds

1 cup (114 g, 4 ounces) shredded
  Monterey Jack cheese

½ cup (120 ml) fat-free milk, warmed

Parsley sprigs, for garnish

Pleasingly smooth and creamy. Exceptionally easy to make. What more could you ask for in a comforting classic? Great taste. It's here, too.

MAKES 4 SERVINGS   **MEDIUM CROCKERY POT**

Combine the water, bouillon, beans, potatoes, and celery seeds in the crockery pot. Cover and cook on LOW or HIGH until the potatoes are very tender, 5 to 6 hours on LOW or 3 to 4 hours on HIGH.

Using a potato masher or hand-held immersible blender, process the potato mixture until smooth, adding the cheese and milk. Garnish with parsley.

PER SERVING: 311 calories, 0.8 g fat, 232 mg sodium, 8.8 g dietary fiber.

QUICK TIP: If you prefer a thinner soup, add milk, ¼ cup (60 ml) at a time.

OLD-WORLD MINESTRONE WITH SHELL PASTA

Sea Scallop Chowder

2 potatoes, peeled and thinly sliced

1 rib celery, thinly sliced

1 carrot, thinly sliced

1 onion, thinly sliced and separated into rings

1 can (10 ounces, 300 ml) clam juice

½ teaspoon dried marjoram leaves

¾ pound (340 g) sea scallops, cut into uniform-size pieces

2 ounces (56 g) cooked lean ham, chopped

1 cup (240 ml) skim milk, warmed

2 teaspoons Worcestershire sauce

Net raves when you make this lightly seasoned shellfish soup. If sea scallops aren't available, get bay scallops and shorten the cooking time slightly so the bays remain tender and succulent.

MAKES 4 SERVINGS   **MEDIUM CROCKERY POT**

Combine the potatoes, celery, carrot, onion, clam juice, and marjoram in the crockery pot. Cover and cook on LOW or HIGH until the potatoes and carrots are tender, 5 to 6 hours on LOW or 3 to 4 hours on HIGH.

Stir in the scallops and ham. Cover and cook until the scallops are cooked through and opaque, about 30 minutes. Stir in the milk and Worcestershire sauce.

PER SERVING: 237 calories, 2.1 g fat, 622 mg sodium, 3 g dietary fiber.

QUICK TIP: *Two slices of lean, cooked deli ham work well in this recipe.*

Turkey-Noodle Soup

2 cans (14 ounces, 420 ml, each) fat-free chicken broth

1 celery stalk, thinly sliced

1 carrot, thinly sliced

1 medium onion, finely chopped

½ pound (228 g) turkey breast, cut into ¾-inch (20 mm) cubes

⅛ teaspoon white pepper

½ teaspoon dried thyme leaves

1 tablespoon white wine vinegar

1 cup medium noodles

½ cup (125 g) peas

Try this soul-warming soup that hits the spot on a cold winter's day. Serve with warm buttermilk biscuits and tossed vegetable salad.

MAKES 4 SERVINGS   **MEDIUM CROCKERY POT**

Combine the broth, celery, carrots, onions, turkey, pepper, thyme, and vinegar in the crockery pot. Cover and cook on LOW until the turkey is tender, 7 to 9 hours (on HIGH, 4 to 6 hours).

Stir in the noodles and peas. Cover and cook until the peas and noodles are done, 5 to 10 minutes.

PER SERVING: About 175 calories, 1 g fat (5% of calories), 0.3 g saturated fat, 56 mg cholesterol, 353 mg sodium, 1.8 g dietary fiber.

COOK'S NOTE: *Chicken breast with thin noodles makes a tasty variation on this dish.*

Summer Vegetable Soup with Basil and Navy Beans

2 teaspoons olive oil

2 onions, cut into thin wedges

2 small (about 4 ounces, 114 g, each) zucchini, halvedlengthwise and sliced ½ inch (13 mm) thick

2 small (about 4 ounces, 114 g, each) yellow squash, halved lengthwise and sliced ½ inch (13 mm) thick

4 cloves garlic, minced

2 cups (460 g) rinsed and drained canned small navy beans

1 can (14 ounces, 400 g) stewed tomatoes

1½ cup (360 ml) reduced-sodium vegetable broth

½ red bell pepper, chopped

¼ teaspoon freshly ground black pepper

½ cup (30 g) snipped fresh basil

Does your garden run over with summer squash and sweet peppers? Here's a super way to savor the bounty. Fresh basil complements the soup's flavor.

MAKES 4 SERVINGS   **MEDIUM CROCKERY POT**

Heat the oil in a nonstick skillet over medium-high heat. Add the onions, zucchini, squash, and garlic, and sauté, stirring, until translucent, 5 to 10 minutes.

Combine the beans, tomatoes, , broth, bell peppers, and beans in the crockery pot. Cover and cook on LOW or HIGH until the the vegetables are tender and the flavors are blended, 4 to 6 hours on LOW or 3 to 4 hours on HIGH.

Stir in the black pepper and basil.

PER SERVING: 284 calories, 3.2 g fat (10% of calories), 0.5 g saturated fat, 0 mg cholesterol, 253 mg sodium, 15 g dietary fiber.

QUICK TIP: To cut fresh leafy herbs like basil, stack them one atop another, roll them up lengthwise, then cut across the roll.

Butternut Squash and Apple Soup

4 potatoes (about 1½ pounds, 680 g), peeled and cut into ¾-inch (20 mm) cubes

1 butternut squash (about 1½ pounds, 680 g), peeled and cut into ¾-inch (20 mm) pieces

1 large McIntosh apple, peeled and coarsely chopped

1 onion, chopped

1 can (14 ounces, 420 ml) reduced-sodium vegetable broth

1 cup (240 ml) water

1 teaspoon pumpkin pie spice

Pinch of white pepper

Here's a light soup with intriguing flavor contrasts—onion, apple, winter squash, and pumpkin pie spice—that's perfect for a spur-of-the-moment dinner. Serve it often in autumn when apples and squash are tiptop and plentiful.

MAKES 4 SERVINGS   **MEDIUM CROCKERY POT**

Combine the potatoes, squash, apples, onions, broth, and water in the crockery pot. Cover and cook on LOW or HIGH until the potatoes are very tender, 5 to 6 hours on LOW or 3 to 4 hours on HIGH.

Stir in the pumpkin pie spice and pepper; let sit for 3 minutes to blend the flavors.

PER SERVING: 251 calories, 0.6 g fat (2% of calories), 0.1 g saturated fat, 0 mg cholesterol, 56 g sodium, 3.9 g dietary fiber.

QUICK TIP: Plumb out of pumpkin pie spice? No matter. You can substitute ½ teaspoon ground ginger and ¼ teaspoon ground nutmeg for the spice combo.

Meatball and Bow Tie Pasta Soup

½ pound (228 g) ground round beef

½ cup (40 g) quick-cooking oats

2 tablespoons dried minced onions

2 teaspoons garlic powder

2 teaspoons dried basil

1 egg white

½ cup (44 g) grated Parmesan cheese

1 can (15 ounces, 426 g) whole
    tomatoes, cut up

3 cups (720 ml) fat-free beef broth

1 cup (180 g) baby carrots, halved
    lengthwise

1 zucchini, halved lengthwise and sliced
    ½ inch (13 mm) thick

4 ounces (114 g) bow tie pasta (farfelle)

Tiny meatballs made with cheese and basil fill this hearty soup with irresistible flavor.

MAKES 4 SERVINGS　　　　　　　　　　**MEDIUM CROCKERY POT**

Combine the beef, oats, 1 teaspoon of the onions, ½ teaspoon of the garlic, ½ teaspoon of the basil, egg white, and ¼ cup (22 g) of the cheese in a bowl. Shape the mixture into sixteen 1-inch-diameter meatballs. Heat a nonstick skillet over medium-high heat. Add the meatballs and cook until brown, about 8 minutes.

Combine the remaining onions, the remaining garlic, the remaining basil, the tomatoes, broth, carrots, zucchini, and meatballs in the crockery pot. Cover and cook on LOW until the meatballs are cooked through and no longer pink and the flavors are blended, 5 to 6 hours.

Cook the pasta according to package directions. Drain well and stir into the meatball-vegetable mixture. Divide among 4 bowls and top each serving with the remaining ¼ cup (22 g) cheese.

PER SERVING: 369 calories, 7.3 g fat (18% of calories), 3.1 g saturated fat, 56 mg cholesterol, 394 mg sodium, 4.9 g dietary fiber.

QUICK TIP: Be sure to form firm meatballs; loosely shaped ones may fall apart during cooking.

Yellow Squash Soup with Watercress

3 russet potatoes, peeled and chopped

1 small yellow squash, sliced

2 cans (14 ounces, 420 ml, each)
    fat-free chicken broth

4 cloves garlic, crushed

½ teaspoon dried marjoram

pinch of white pepper

1 cup (80 g) watercress

Pale yellow mild squash and deep green peppery-tasting watercress play well together in this light soup, which makes for a delightful first course. Or if soup and sandwiches are to your liking, pair it with seafood salad tucked into pita pocket bread.

MAKES 4 SERVINGS　　　　　　　　　　**MEDIUM CROCKERY POT**

Combine the potatoes, squash, broth, garlic, marjoram, and white pepper in the crockery pot. Cover and cook on LOW or HIGH just until the potatoes are tender, 4 to 6 hours on LOW or 2 to 4 hours on HIGH.

Divide the soup among 4 bowls. Top each serving with ¼ cup (80 g) watercress.

PER SERVING: 139 calories, 0.3 g fat, 153 mg sodium, 2.7 g dietary fiber.

QUICK TIP: If you're in a big hurry, skip peeling the potatoes. But expect to see flecks of skin floating in the broth.

MEATBALL AND BOW TIE PASTA SOUP

Summer Squash Soup with Lemon Grass

1 can (14 ounces, 420 ml) Oriental broth or chicken or vegetable broth

2 cups water

2 small zucchini, halved lengthwise and sliced

1 medium yellow squash, halved lengthwise and sliced

1 leek, white part only, sliced

1 medium onion, halved lengthwise and thinly sliced

3 cloves garlic, pressed

1 stalk lemon grass, halved

½ teaspoon Thai seasoning

¼ teaspoon crushed red pepper flakes

6 medium kale leaves, chopped

Lemon grass imparts an enticing lemony fragrance to this pleasantly nippy yet delicate Thai-spiced soup.

MAKES 4 SERVINGS　　　　　　　　　**MEDIUM CROCKERY POT**

Combine the broth, water, zucchini, squash, leek, onion, garlic, lemon grass, Thai seasoning, and pepper flakes in the crockery pot. Cover and cook on LOW for 5 to 9 hours or on HIGH for 3½ to 5 hours. Discard the lemon grass. Stir in the kale. Cover and cook until the kale is wilted, 5 to 10 minutes.

PER SERVING: About 73 calories, 0.6 g fat (6% of calories), 0.1 g saturated fat, 0 mg cholesterol, 538 mg sodium, 2.9 g dietary fiber.

COOK'S NOTE: Lemon grass is available in Asian specialty markets and many supermarkets. If you can't find any, substitute a 2-inch piece of lemon peel.

Vegetable–Rice Soup with Maple Bacon

4 slices maple-cured bacon

¾ cup (150 g) brown rice

2 cans (14 ounces, 420 ml, each) fat-free beef broth

1 can (14 ounces (400 g)) diced tomatoes

1 cup frozen cut green beans

1 onion, chopped

1 rib celery, thinly sliced

3 cloves garlic, minced

1 sprig fresh thyme

¼ teaspoon freshly ground black pepper

¼ cup (15 g) snipped fresh dill, for garnish

This superb and classic home-style soup is brimming with green beans and fresh thyme as well as the usual tomatoes and rice. A smidgen of maple-cured bacon perks up the flavor.

MAKES 4 SERVINGS　　　　　　　　　**MEDIUM CROCKERY POT**

Cook the bacon in a nonstick skillet over medium-high heat until brown and crisp. Remove to a paper-towel-lined plate, and drain the fat from the skillet. Crumble the bacon and set aside.

Return the skillet to the heat, and add the rice. Cook, stirring, just until the rice starts to brown, about 10 minutes.

Combine the broth, rice, tomatoes, beans, onion, celery, garlic, thyme, and pepper in the crockery pot. Cover and cook on LOW until the rice is tender, 3 to 4 hours. Stir in the bacon. Divide among 4 bowls and top each serving with the dill.

PER SERVING: 210 calories, 3.5 g fat, 238 mg sodium, 3.5 g dietary fiber.

QUICK TIP: Cut the dill with scissors, discarding the stem.

Shrimp-Rice Soup

2 cans (14 ounces, 420 ml, each) fat-free chicken broth

1 small onion, finely chopped

1 celery stalk, thinly sliced

⅛ teaspoon white pepper

¼ cup brown rice

½ pound (228 g) medium shrimp, shelled, deveined, and cut into thirds

A light, delicately seasoned soup that makes a delicious first course—perfect for a luncheon or dinner.

MAKES 4 SERVINGS   **MEDIUM CROCKERY POT**

Combine the broth, onion, celery, pepper, and rice in the crockery pot. Cover and cook on LOW for 6 to 8 hours or on HIGH for 4 to 6 hours. During the last hour of cooking, stir in the shrimp. Cover and cook until the shrimp are cooked through and tender, about 1 hour.

PER SERVING: About 129 calories, 1.3 g fat (9% of calories), 0.3 g saturated fat, 86 mg cholesterol, 397 mg sodium, 0.5 g dietary fiber.

COOK'S NOTE: To make **CHICKEN-RICE SOUP,** replace the shrimp with cubed chicken breast. Add the chicken along with the broth and other ingredients.

Thymely Vegetable Soup with Ziti

2 cups water

1 medium onion, chopped

½ cup dried lentils, rinsed

1 small carrot, thinly sliced

¼ teaspoon celery seed

2½ teaspoons brown sugar

¼ teaspoon dried marjoram

¼ teaspoon dried thyme leaves

⅛ teaspoon freshly ground black pepper

2 cloves garlic, minced

1 can (14 ounces, 420 ml) fat-free chicken or vegetable broth

1 can (15 ounces, 426 g) crushed tomatoes

½ medium zucchini, cut in half lengthwise and thinly sliced

½ cup (75 g) frozen corn

2 tablespoons white wine vinegar

½ cup (114 g) ziti

½ cup (42 g) grated Parmesan or Romano cheese

Here's a dish with plenty of herbal flavor and just the right amount of zip. Serve with crusty rustic or French bread.

MAKES 4 SERVINGS   **LARGE CROCKERY POT**

Mix the water, onions, lentils, carrots, and celery seed in the crockery pot. Stir in the sugar, marjoram, thyme, pepper, garlic, broth, tomatoes, zucchini, corn, and vinegar. Cover and cook on LOW for 6 to 8 hours or on HIGH for 4 to 5 hours. During the last hour of cooking, stir in the ziti. Cover and cook until the ziti are al dente, 10 to 30 minutes. Divide the soup among 4 bowls, and sprinkle each serving with 2 tablespoons of the cheese.

PER SERVING: About 288 calories, 4.4 g fat (14% of calories), 2.5 g saturated fat, 10 mg cholesterol, 659 mg sodium, 3.5 g dietary fiber.

COOK'S NOTE: This soup is best when served freshly made.

Vegetable Soup for All Seasons

1 teaspoon olive oil

2 leeks, white part only, thinly sliced

6 cloves garlic, minced

3 cans (14 ounces, 420 ml, each)
    fat-free chicken broth

3 white potatoes, peeled and chopped

2 white turnips, peeled and shredded

1 small yellow squash, cubed

1 carrot, shredded

2 bay leaves

¼ teaspoon white pepper

1 small green bell pepper, chopped,
    for garnish

Fall, winter, and summer vegetables star in this mostly vegetable soup. Can't find white turnips? Then substitute rutabagas, also known as swedes or Swedish turnips. To make a vegetarian version, replace the chicken broth with vegetable broth.

MAKES 8 SERVINGS   **LARGE CROCKERY POT**

Heat the oil in a nonstick skillet over medium-high heat. Add the leeks and garlic, and sauté, stirring, until lightly browned.

Combine the leek mixture, broth, potatoes, turnips, squash, carrots, bay leaves, and white pepper in the crockery pot. Cover and cook on LOW until the potatoes are tender, 5 to 6 hours. Discard the bay leaves.

Divide among 8 bowls. Garnish each serving with the bell peppers.

PER SERVING: 130 calories, 0.8 g fat, 133 mg sodium, 3.2 g dietary fiber.

QUICK TIP: Leeks can be a sandy lot. To clean them, cut off the root ends and trim the tops. Split lengthwise and swish in lots of cold water.

Tomato-Basil Soup with Ditalini Pasta

1 can (28 ounces, 800 g) crushed
    tomatoes

1 clove garlic, minced

1 small onion, finely chopped

1 small carrot, finely shredded

1 celery stalk, thinly sliced

½ cup (120 ml) vegetable broth

1 teaspoon sugar

1 bay leaf

1 tablespoon dry sherry

⅛ teaspoon black pepper

4 fresh basil leaves, snipped

1 cup (228 g) ditalini or orzo

1 cup (240 ml) evaporated skim milk

A hearty tomato classic that packs plenty of flavor and uses small pasta instead of rice.

MAKES 4 SERVINGS   **MEDIUM CROCKERY POT**

Combine tomatoes, garlic, onions, carrots, celery, broth, sugar, bay leaf, sherry, and pepper in the crockery pot. Cover and cook on LOW for 6 to 8 hours or on HIGH for 4 to 6 hours. Discard bay leaf.

Stir in the basil and ditalini. Cover and cook for 10 minutes. Stir in milk. Cover and cook until the ditalini are tender and the soup hot, 5 to 30 minutes.

PER SERVING: About 250 calories, 0.7 g fat (2% of calories), 0.2 g saturated fat, 2.3 mg cholesterol, 458 mg sodium, 4.3 g dietary fiber.

COOK'S NOTE: Ditalini cook quickly; be careful not to overcook.

VEGETABLE SOUP FOR ALL SEASONS

Turkey Vegetable Soup with Annelini

2 cans (14 ounces, 420 ml, each) fat-free chicken broth

½ cup (120 ml) water

6 ounces (170 g) boneless, skinless turkey breast, cut into ½-inch (13 mm) cubes

1 potato, cut into ½-inch (13 mm) cubes

2 cups (300 g) frozen mixed Italian-style vegetables (a combination of broccoli, flat green beans, and zucchini), thawed

½ teaspoon dried sage

¼ teaspoon freshly ground black pepper

1 cup annelini pasta

A frozen Italian-style vegetable mix cuts chopping time to practically nothing in this flavorful one-pot soup.

MAKES 4 SERVINGS   **MEDIUM CROCKERY POT**

Combine the broth, water, turkey, and potato in the crockery pot. Cover and cook on LOW until the turkey is cooked through and the potatoes are tender, 5 to 6 hours.

Stir in the mixed vegetables, sage, pepper, and ditalini. Cover and cook on LOW until the vegetables are tender, ½ to 1 hour.

PER SERVING: 233 calories, 0.8 g fat (3% of calories), 0.2 g saturated fat, 35 mg cholesterol, 190 mg sodium, 2.6 g dietary fiber.

QUICK TIP: In this recipe, peel the potatoes or simply give them a good scrubbing. The choice is yours to make.

Potato Cheddar-Cheese Soup

6 large or 10 medium potatoes, peeled and cut into 1-inch (2.5 cm) cubes

½ cup (120 ml) low-sodium vegetable broth

1 cup water

1 large onion, finely chopped

½ teaspoon garlic powder

⅛ teaspoon white pepper

2 cups (480 ml) skim milk

1 cup (110 g) shredded sharp or extra-sharp Cheddar cheese

Paprika, for garnish

A thick, cheddary soup to die for! Accompany it with vegetable crudités (carrots, celery, cauliflower, sweet red pepper and broccoli) and serve chocolate chip muffins for dessert.

MAKES 4 SERVINGS   **MEDIUM CROCKERY POT**

Place the potatoes, broth, water, onions, and garlic powder in the crockery pot. Cover and cook on LOW until the potatoes are tender, 7 to 9 hours (on HIGH, 4 to 6 hours).

Using a potato masher or a hand-held blender, mash the potatoes, stirring in the pepper and the milk a little at a time. Mix in the cheese and cook until the cheese has melted, about 5 minutes. Add more milk if needed. Divide the soup among 4 bowls; garnish each serving with paprika.

PER SERVING: About 350 calories, 10 g fat (25% of calories), 6.2 g saturated fat, 32 mg cholesterol, 265 mg sodium, 4 g dietary fiber.

COOK'S NOTE: Nonfat Cheddar cheese will work in this recipe, but it won't have the flavor impact.

Rutabaga Soup with Nutmeg

2 medium onions, chopped

1 stalk celery, chopped

3 cups of 1-inch (2.5 cm) cubes of
   peeled potatoes

2 cups of 1-inch (2.5 cm) cubes of
   peeled rutabagas

2 cans (14 ounces, 420 ml, each)
   fat-free chicken broth

2 cloves garlic, minced

⅛ teaspoon white pepper

⅓ cup (80 ml) skim milk

1 teaspoon ground nutmeg

Snipped fresh flat parsley, for garnish

The Swedish turnip or rutabaga, once known as the swede, plus some potatoes equal an outstanding creamy soup.

MAKES 8 SERVINGS **MEDIUM CROCKERY POT**

Combine the onions, celery, potatoes, rutabagas, broth, garlic, and pepper in the crockery pot. Cover and cook on HIGH until the vegetables are tender, 4 to 6 hours. Using a hand-held blender, puree the vegetables. Stir in the milk.

Divide the soup among 8 bowls. Sprinkle each serving with ⅛ teaspoon nutmeg, and garnish with the parsley.

PER SERVING: About 108 calories, 0.2 g fat (2% of calories), 0.1 g saturated fat, 0.2 mg cholesterol, 188 mg sodium, 2.8 g dietary fiber.

COOK'S NOTE: If rutabagas aren't readily available, substitute white turnips.

Smoky Pinto Bean and Potato Soup

1 medium onion, chopped

2 medium red potatoes, cut into
   ½-inch (13 mm) cubes

2 carrots, thinly sliced

1 celery stalk, thinly sliced

1 can (14 ounces, 400 g) pinto beans,
   rinsed and drained

2 cans (14 ounces, 420 ml, each) fat-free
   beef broth

2 cloves garlic, chopped

½ teaspoon cumin seed

¼ teaspoon black pepper

1 teaspoon mesquite smoke flavoring

1 tablespoon white wine vinegar

¼ pound (228 g) chopped smoked
   sausage (optional)

Here's a serious hunger-stopper that's packed with fiber-rich potatoes, carrots and beans, and intriguing cumin-mesquite flavor, as well.

MAKES 6 SERVINGS **MEDIUM CROCKERY POT**

Combine the onions, potatoes, carrots, celery, beans, sausage, if you wish, and broth in the crockery pot. Stir in the garlic, cumin, pepper, smoke flavoring, and vinegar. Cover and cook on HIGH until the vegetables are tender, 3½ to 5 hours.

PER SERVING: About 137 calories, 1.7 g fat (11% of calories), 0.3 g saturated fat, 0 mg cholesterol, 236 mg sodium, 4.2 g dietary fiber.

RED BEAN AND SALAMI SOUP

Red Bean and Salami Soup

2 teaspoons olive oil

1 small onion, chopped

6 cloves garlic, minced

1 small white eggplant, chopped

2 cans (14 ounces, 420 ml, each) fat-free beef broth

1 can (15 ounces, 426 g) diced tomatoes

1 can (15 ounces, 426 g) red kidney beans, rinsed and drained

1 small zucchini, sliced

2 ounces (57 g) hard salami, chopped

½ teaspoon freshly ground black pepper

4 sprigs thyme

Just a little salami provides unique flavor in this simple soup. I've used red kidney beans, but pinto or a combination of kidney and pinto beans would be just as tasty. If your family and friends are anything like mine, they'll request this basic soup often. But don't tell them how easy it is to toss together.

MAKES 6 SERVINGS   **MEDIUM CROCKERY POT**

Heat the oil in a large nonstick skillet over medium-high heat. Add the onions, garlic, and eggplant. Sauté, stirring frequently, until the eggplant is lightly browned, about 10 minutes. Add ¼ cup of the broth and stir to deglaze the skillet.

Combine the eggplant mixture, remaining broth, tomatoes with juice, beans, zucchini, salami, pepper, and thyme in the crockery pot. Cover and cook on LOW or HIGH until the vegetables are tender and the flavors are blended, 5 to 6 hours on LOW or 3 to 4 hours on HIGH. Discard the thyme sprigs.

PER SERVING: 179 calories, 5.3 g fat, 276 mg sodium, 6.8 g dietary fiber.

QUICK TIP: If thyme sprigs are young and tender, mince and add them to the soup. If they're woody oldsters, use them whole and discard them after cooking.

Tomato-Tortilla Soup

4 cups (800 g) crushed tomatoes

1¼ cups (300 ml) vegetable broth

2 medium onions, finely chopped

3 cloves garlic, minced

2 dried cayenne peppers, minced, or 2 teaspoons crushed red pepper flakes

1 tablespoon dried parsley

6 corn tortillas, cut into ¾-inch (20 mm) strips

Nonstick olive oil spray

1 cup (4 ounces, 114 g) shredded Monterey Jack cheese

Crisp flat-bread tops a peppery-hot, south-of-the-border-style soup. Get ready for a superb, palate-stimulating experience!

MAKES 6 SERVINGS   **MEDIUM CROCKERY POT**

Combine the tomatoes, broth, onions, garlic, peppers, and parsley in the crockery pot. Cover and cook on LOW for 7 to 9 hours or on HIGH for 3½ to 5 hours.

Place the tortillas on a baking sheet, and mist them with the olive oil spray. Broil them until they're crisp and golden, about 5 minutes.

Divide the soup among 6 bowls, and top each serving with tortilla strips and cheese.

PER SERVING: About 210 calories, 6.6 g fat (28% of calories), 3.7 g saturated fat, 17 mg cholesterol, 421 mg sodium, 3.7 g dietary fiber.

COOK'S NOTE: Toasted flour tortillas or crisp, broken taco shells can replace the corn tortillas.

Pimiento-Mushroom Soup

2 cans (14 ounces, 420 ml, each) reduced-fat chicken or vegetable broth

1 tablespoon white wine vinegar

1 bay leaf

8 ounces (228 g) mushrooms, sliced

2 celery stalks, sliced

2 carrots, sliced

1 jar (4 ounces, 114 g) pimientos, drained

1 medium onion, chopped

Sprigs of cilantro, for garnish

Mushroom aficionados take note: This attractive, light soup goes together almost as fast as you can say pimiento-mushroom.

MAKES 4 SERVINGS **MEDIUM CROCKERY POT**

Combine the broth, vinegar, bay leaf, mushrooms, celery, carrots, pimientos, and onions in the crockery pot. Cover and cook on LOW for 6 to 8 hours or on HIGH for 4 to 6 hours. Discard the bay leaf. Divide the soup among 4 bowls, and garnish each serving with the cilantro.

PER SERVING: About 159 calories, 1.3 g fat (6% of calories), 0.1 g saturated fat, 0 mg cholesterol, 378 mg sodium, 6 g dietary fiber.

COOK'S NOTE: This soup keeps nicely in the refrigerator for a day or two.

Tomato-Cheese Tortellini Soup

1 can (28 ounces, 800 g) whole plum tomatoes, cut up

2 cans (14 ounces, 420 ml, each) vegetable broth or fat-free chicken broth

1 cup sliced scallions

1 cup (171 g) chopped fresh or frozen green peppers

½ teaspoon dried oregano

1 tablespoon snipped fresh basil or ½ teaspoon dried

1 tablespoon white wine vinegar

2 cups (1 pound, 455 g) frozen tricolor cheese tortellini

Stuffed pasta gets a "souper" role in this robust one-dish meal.

MAKES 8 SERVINGS **MEDIUM CROCKERY POT**

Combine the tomatoes, broth, scallions, peppers, oregano, basil, and vinegar in the crockery pot. Cover and cook on LOW for 6 to 8 hours or on HIGH for 4 to 5 hours.

During the last hour of cooking, stir in the tortellini. Cover and cook until the tortellini are tender and hot, about 75 minutes.

PER SERVING: About 220 calories, 7.7 g fat (31% of calories), 4 g saturated fat, 50 mg cholesterol, 402 mg sodium, 1.8 g dietary fiber.

COOK'S NOTES: Fresh tortellini will also work in this recipe; allow 45 to 60 minutes for them to cook.
The soup is best eaten fresh, but will keep for up to 3 days in the refrigerator.

Vegetables
and Sides

Acorn Squash with Pepper-Rice Stuffing

1 acorn squash (about 1½ pounds, 680 g)

¼ cup (50 g) long-grain rice

1 carrot, coarsely shredded

1 small sweet green pepper, chopped

2 cloves garlic, minced

1 teaspoon turmeric

½ cup (120 ml) water

½ cup (120 ml) vegetable broth

¼ cup (60 g) nonfat sour cream, for garnish

¼ cup (20 g) snipped fresh parsley, for garnish

This quick-and-easy vegetarian dish is long on flavor, short on fat.

MAKES 4 SIDE DISH SERVINGS   **LARGE RECTANGULAR CROCKERY POT**

Cut the squash in half lengthwise and remove the seeds. Combine the rice, carrots, peppers, garlic and turmeric, and spoon the mixture into the squash cavities.

Pour the water into the crockery pot, and add the squash halves, cavity-sides up. Pour the broth into the rice mixture in each cavity. Cook on LOW until the squash and rice are tender, 5 to 7 hours. Serve garnished with the sour cream and parsley.

PER SERVING: About 136 calories, 0.4 g fat (2% of calories), 0.1 g saturated fat, 0 mg cholesterol, 34 mg sodium, 3.3 g dietary fiber.

COOK'S NOTE: To serve this as a main dish, top each helping with shredded Cheddar cheese or chopped nuts, and allow ½ squash per serving. (To cook 2 small squashes at once, use an electric skillet set to simmer, instead of a crockery pot.)

Black Bean and Corn Chili

1 can (14–19 ounces, 400-540 g) black beans, rinsed and drained

1 can (28 ounces, 800 g) tomatoes, cut up

1 large green bell pepper, chopped

2 large onions, chopped

1½ cups (211 g) corn

1 chili pepper, seeded and chopped

4 cloves garlic, minced

2 tablespoons chili powder

2 teaspoons ground cumin

1 teaspoon dried oregano

Create a stir with knockout chili that's full of beans and other healthful vegetables.

MAKES: 4 SERVINGS   **MEDIUM CROCKERY POT**

Combine the beans, tomatoes, bell pepper, onions, corn, chili pepper, garlic, chili powder, cumin and oregano in the crockery pot. Cover and cook on LOW or HIGH until the flavors are blended, 5 to 6 hours on LOW or 3 to 4 hours on HIGH.

PER SERVING: 491 calories, 8.2 g fat (14% of calories), 1.5 g saturated fat, 0.6 mg cholesterol, 179 mg sodium, 14.8 g dietary fiber.

Black-Bean- and Corn-Stuffed Peppers

½ cup (100 g) rice, cooked

½ cup (114 g) canned black beans, rinsed and drained

3 cloves garlic, minced

½ cup (80 g) sliced scallions

½ cup (75 g) frozen corn

2 plum tomatoes, diced

2 sprigs of cilantro, snipped

2 sprigs of parsley, snipped, or 2 teaspoons dried

3 fresh basil leaves, snipped, or ½ teaspoon dried

⅛ teaspoon white pepper

½ teaspoon chili powder

4 large sweet green peppers, with tops, membranes, and seeds removed

½ cup (100 g) crushed tomatoes

½ cup (120 ml) water

2 ounces (57 g) Monterey Jack or Cheddar cheese, shredded

A delicious vegetarian dish that the whole family will love. It's packed with all the right stuff and makes a meal in itself.

MAKES 4 SERVINGS **MEDIUM CROCKERY POT**

Combine the rice, beans, garlic, scallions, corn, diced tomatoes, cilantro, parsley, basil, white pepper, and chili powder in a bowl. Toss to mix well. Divide the rice mixture into 4 portions, and spoon a portion into each of the sweet peppers.

Pour the tomatoes and water into a crockery pot; place the peppers, upright, in the crockery pot. Cover and cook on LOW for 4 to 6 hours. Transfer the peppers to serving plates, and top each with a generous spoonful of hot tomatoes and shredded cheese.

PER SERVING: About 203 calories, 4.9 g fat (21% of calories), 2.8 g saturated fat, 13 mg cholesterol, 166 mg sodium, 3.7 g dietary fiber.

COOK'S NOTE: You can stuff these peppers the night before, if you wish. Place them in your crockery pot's removable ceramic bowl, cover it, and refrigerate the entire thing until about 30 minutes before you're ready to start the crockery pot. Then remove the bowl from the refrigerator and let it sit on the counter. After 30 minutes, cook the peppers according to the recipe directions.

Slow-Cooked Barbecue Sauce

1 can (15 ounces, 426 g) crushed tomatoes

½ cup (120 ml) water

1 medium onion, chopped

¼ teaspoon chili powder

¼ teaspoon paprika

2 tablespoons sugar or brown sugar

1 tablespoon Dijon mustard

1 teaspoon Worcestershire sauce

2 tablespoons cider vinegar or red wine vinegar

A basic sauce with a tomato-onion flavor and just a hint of sweetness. It's great for jazzing up grilled meats and poultry. Feel free to use it liberally; it's low in fat and sodium.

YIELDS ABOUT 2½ CUPS (600 ML) **MEDIUM CROCKERY POT**

Mix the tomatoes, water, onions, chili, paprika, sugar, mustard, Worcestershire, and vinegar in a crockery pot. Cover and cook on LOW for 4 to 6 hours.

PER ¼ CUP (60 ML): About 32 calories, 0.1 g fat (3% of calories), 0 g saturated fat, 0 mg cholesterol, 148 mg sodium, 1 g dietary fiber.

COOK'S NOTE: The sauce will keep in the refrigerator for up to a week.

Stuffed Zucchini

1 medium zucchini, halved lengthwise, with seeds removed

1 cup (240 ml) low-sodium tomato sauce

1 tablespoon red wine vinegar

1 small onion, finely chopped

2 cloves garlic, chopped

¼ cup (50 g) brown rice

¼ cup (20 g) snipped fresh parsley

4 basil leaves, snipped

⅛ teaspoon black pepper

2 tablespoons toasted pine nuts, for garnish

Gardeners take note: Here's yet another tasty way to use the summer's bounty. Medium-sized produce make the best squash boats.

MAKES 4 SERVINGS　　　　　　**LARGE RECTANGULAR CROCKERY POT**

Place the zucchini in the bottom of the crockery pot. In a measuring cup, combine the tomato sauce and vinegar.

In a bowl, combine the onions, garlic, rice, parsley, basil, pepper, and 2 tablespoons of the tomato sauce mixture. Spoon the rice mixture into the zucchini "boats." Top with the remaining tomato mixture. Cover and cook on LOW until the rice is tender, 4 to 6 hours. Garnish with the pine nuts.

PER SERVING: 89 calories, 0.5 g fat (5% of calories), 0.1 g saturated fat, 0 mg cholesterol, 22 mg sodium, 2 g dietary fiber.

COOK'S NOTE: To toast pine nuts (also called pignolias or piñons), place them in a small nonstick skillet. Then warm them over medium heat, shaking the skillet occasionally, until they're golden, about 5 minutes.

Chili-Stuffed Chayote Squash

3 chayote squash or small zucchini, halved

1 tamarillo, peeled and sliced

1 small onion, quartered

4 cloves garlic, halved

2 tablespoons minced fresh sage

1 chipotle chili, seeded and chopped

2 tablespoons recaito sauce

¼ cup (60 ml) water

6 sprigs fresh cilantro, chopped

6 tablespoons fat-free sour cream

Chipotle chili revs up the flavor — and the heat — of the mild, almost bland, chayote squash in this colorful recipe. Tame the flame with sour cream.

MAKES 6 SERVINGS　　　　　　**MEDIUM CROCKERY POT**

Scoop the pulp from the squash, reserving the pulp and leaving ½- to ¼-inch (13 to 20 mm)shells. Combine the pulp, tamarillo, onions, garlic, sage, and chipotle in a food processor. Process until finely chopped. Stir in the recaito sauce. Spoon into the squash shells.

Arrange in the crockery pot. Cover and cook LOW or HIGH until the squash is tender, 5 to 9 hours (on LOW) or 3½ to 5 hours (on HIGH). Serve topped with the cilantro and sour cream.

PER SERVING: 65 calories, 0.3 g fat, 24 mg sodium, 2.4 g dietary fiber.

QUICK TIPS: Chipotle chilies are smoked, dried jalapeño peppers. If you can't find them, substitute another dried hot pepper. Look for recaito sauce, which is similar to sofrito, in the Hispanic section of large supermarkets.

STUFFED ZUCCHINI

Simmered Spaghetti Sauce

1 teaspoon olive oil

1 can (6 ounces, 170 g) low-sodium tomato paste

1 can (28 ounces, 800 g) Italian plum tomatoes

3 medium onions, finely chopped

4 cloves garlic, minced

1 celery stalk, finely chopped

½ cup (120 ml) water

¼ teaspoon black pepper

¼ teaspoon chili powder

¼ teaspoon ground allspice

1 tablespoon sugar

¼ teaspoon dried thyme leaves

1 bay leaf

⅓ cup (27 g) snipped fresh parsley, or 1 tablespoon dried

⅓ cup (40 g) snipped fresh basil, or 1 tablespoon dried

Slow simmering blends the flavors in this superb chunky sauce. Serve it over your favorite pasta and enjoy it with warmed, crusty Italian bread and a tossed salad topped with red-wine vinaigrette.

YIELDS ABOUT 6 CUPS (1.3 L)   **MEDIUM CROCKERY POT**

Mix the oil, tomato paste, tomatoes, onions, garlic, celery, and water in the crockery pot. Stir in the pepper, chili powder, allspice, sugar, thyme, and bay leaf. Cook on LOW for 8 to 10 hours. Discard the bay leaf. Stir in the parsley and basil during the last half-hour of cooking. Serve over your favorite spaghetti.

PER ½ CUP (120 L): About 113 calories, 0.6 g fat (5% of calories), 0.1 g saturated fat, 0 mg cholesterol, 157 mg sodium, 1.9 g dietary fiber.

COOK'S NOTE: For a meat sauce, brown ½ pound (228g) of extra lean ground meat, and add it to the crockery pot for all-day cooking.

Pierogies in Pepper-Shallot Sauce

1 can (28 ounces, 800 g) crushed tomatoes

1 shallot, thinly sliced

1 cup (171 g) chopped sweet green peppers

½ teaspoon olive oil

½ tablespoon red wine vinegar

½ teaspoon Italian herb seasoning

½ teaspoon black pepper

1 pound (455 g) potato-filled pierogies, fresh or frozen

Here a chunky, robust sauce enhances the less intense flavors of potato-filled pierogies.

MAKES 6 SERVINGS   **LARGE CROCKERY POT**

Combine the tomatoes, shallots, peppers, oil, vinegar, seasoning, and black pepper in the crockery pot. Cover and cook on LOW for 5 to 9 hours or on HIGH for 3½ to 5 hours. Add the pierogies. Cover and cook for 1 hour.

PER SERVING: About 179 calories, 2.1 g fat (10% of calories), 0.7 g saturated fat, 10 mg cholesterol, 522 mg sodium, 4.2 g dietary fiber.

COOK'S NOTE: Pierogies are Polish filled dumplings. Thaw frozen pierogies before adding them to the sauce.

New-Fashioned Baked Beans

3 cups (600 g) crushed tomatoes

2 cans (15 ounces, 426 g, each) great northern beans

½ pound (228 g) Canadian bacon, cut into ¼-inch (6 mm) cubes

1 medium onion, minced

¼ cup brown sugar

1 tablespoon coarse brown mustard

2 tablespoons red wine vinegar

½ teaspoon hickory smoke flavoring

This incredibly easy and great-tasting recipe makes enough for a small crowd. Why not simmer up a potful for your next potluck supper?

MAKES 10 SERVINGS   **MEDIUM CROCKERY POT**

Combine the tomatoes, beans, bacon, onions, sugar, mustard, vinegar, and smoke flavoring in the crockery pot. Cover and cook on LOW for 7 to 9 hours.

PER SERVING: About 202 calories, 2.2 g fat (10% of calories), 0.7 g saturated fat, 11 mg cholesterol, 427 mg sodium, 5.2 g dietary fiber.

COOK'S NOTE: These spicy-sweet beans keep in the refrigerator for 3 to 4 days. Small white beans or white kidney beans can be substituted for the great northerns.

Fast Parsley Potatoes

1 cup (240 ml) fat-free chicken broth

4 large potatoes, cut into ¾-inch (20 mm) cubes

1 teaspoon olive oil

¼ cup (20 g) finely snipped fresh parsley

¼ teaspoon freshly ground black pepper

Always popular and never a hassle, these potatoes will complement most meat, fish, or poultry main dishes.

MAKES: 4 SERVINGS   **MEDIUM CROCKERY POT**

Combine the broth and potatoes in the crockery pot. Cover and cook on LOW or HIGH until the potatoes are very tender, 5 to 6 hours on LOW or 3 to 4 hours on HIGH.

Using a slotted spoon, remove the potatoes to a serving bowl. Drizzle with the oil and top with the parsley and pepper.

PER SERVING: 141 calories, 1.3 g fat (8% of calories), 0.2 g saturated fat, 0 mg cholesterol, 52 mg sodium, 2.7 g dietary fiber.

QUICK TIP: To snip parsley quickly, place it in a small cup. Then holding scissors with the blades pointed into the cup, snip until the parsley is cut to the desired degree of fineness.

Picante Lentil Sauce

1 can (28 ounces, 800 g) crushed
   tomatoes

¼ cup (25 g) lentils, rinsed

2 medium onions, chopped

5 cloves garlic, minced

1 teaspoon sugar

½ teaspoon cumin seeds

1 fresh green chili, minced

½ cup (120 ml) medium-hot
   picante sauce

Lentils and cumin impart complex earthy flavors to this south-of-the-border-style sauce. Enjoy it over omelets, burritos, spaghetti squash, pasta, or rice.

YIELDS ABOUT 4 CUPS (960 ML)   **MEDIUM CROCKERY POT**

Combine the tomatoes, lentils, onions, garlic, sugar, cumin, chili, and picante sauce in the crockery pot. Cover and cook on LOW until the lentils are tender, 6 to 8 hours.

PER CUP (240 ML): About 158 calories, 0.8 g fat (4% of calories), 0 g saturated fat, 0 mg cholesterol, 532 mg sodium, 4.9 g dietary fiber.

COOK'S NOTE: The sauce can be cooked on LOW for up to 10 hours.

Orange Rice

2 cups (480 ml) fat-free chicken broth

1 cup (200 g) wild pecan rice

1 tablespoon minced gingerroot

2 teaspoons grated orange peel

Sometimes, simple is tastiest. This unassuming rice dish gets its special flavor from fresh ginger and grated orange peel.

MAKES 4 SERVINGS   **MEDIUM CROCKERY POT**

Combine the broth, rice, gingerroot, and orange peel in the crockery pot. Cover and cook on LOW until the rice is tender and the liquid has been absorbed, 1½ to 2 hours.

PER SERVING: 68 calories, 0.1 g fat, 86 mg sodium, 0.3 g dietary fiber.

QUICK TIP: Other aromatic rices, such as basmati, jasmati, and texmati, can be submitted for the wild pecan rice. Cooking times will be about the same.

Balsamic Beets

6 medium beets (about ½ pound, 228 g, each), peeled, with roots and tops removed

3 cups (720 ml) water (or enough to cover the beets in the crockery pot)

1 tablespoon balsamic vinegar

1 bay leaf

FOR CHERVIL BUTTER:

¼ cup (57 g) butter, melted

2 teaspoons dried chervil

FOR HORSERADISH MUSTARD:

2 tablespoons horseradish

2 tablespoons Dijon mustard

Beet buffs take note: These burgundy-colored roots have a natural affinity for chervil butter and horseradish mustard.

MAKES 6 SERVINGS **LARGE CROCKERY POT**

Place the beets in the crockery pot. Add water, vinegar, bay leaf. Cover and cook on LOW until the beets are tender, 6 to 8 hours. Discard the bay leaf. Drain and slice beets; serve with the chervil butter or horseradish mustard.

PER SERVING: About 102 calories, 0.3 g fat (3% of calories), 0.1 g saturated fat, 0 mg cholesterol, 167 mg sodium, 7 g dietary fiber.

COOK'S NOTES: To ensure even color, turn the beets once or twice during cooking.

To make chervil butter, combine the melted butter and the dried chervil.

To make horseradish mustard, mix the horseradish with the Dijon mustard.

Creamy Turnips with Cheese

1¼ cups (300 ml) fat-free chicken broth

1 pound (445 g) turnips, peeled and cut into ½-inch (13 mm) pieces

1 pound (445 g) potatoes, peeled and cut into ½-inch (13 mm) pieces

½ cup (121 g) nonfat ricotta cheese

¼ (28 g) cup shredded sharp cheddar cheese

¼ teaspoon white pepper

Paprika, garnish

Delight family, friends, even finicky eaters with this smooth dish of potatoes, turnips, and two cheeses.

MAKES: 4 SERVINGS **MEDIUM CROCKERY POT**

Combine the broth, turnips, and potatoes in the crockery pot. Cover and cook on LOW or HIGH until the vegetables are very tender, 5 to 6 hours on LOW or 3 to 4 hours on HIGH.

Using a potato masher, a hand-held immersion blender, or a hand-held mixer, mash the turnip–potato mixture, blending in the ricotta cheese, cheddar, and white pepper. Garnish each serving with the paprika and serve.

PER SERVING: 169 calories, 1.2 g fat (6% of calories), 0.5 g saturated fat, 5.3 mg cholesterol, 189 mg sodium, 4.3 g dietary fiber.

QUICK TIP: The peak season for turnips is October through February. For tender, sweet-tasting turnips, get young ones—they'll be small and heavy for their size. Oldsters tend to be large and woody and have a strong flavor.

SZECHUAN-SPICED RICE WITH CHINESE VEGETABLES

Szechuan-Spiced Rice with Chinese Vegetables

1 can (14 ounces, 420 ml) fat-free
   chicken broth

1 cup (200 g) brown rice

2 teaspoons reduced-sodium soy sauce

1 can (8 ounce, 228 g) sliced water
   chestnuts, rinsed and drained

1 can (8 ounces, 228 g) sliced bamboo
   shoots, rinsed and drained

1½ teaspoons Szechuan seasoning

1 teaspoon crushed garlic

Rice is nice with a little spice. Here, Szechuan seasoning — a blend of ginger, black pepper, red pepper, garlic, and paprika — perks up mild-tasting rice. Chinese vegetables add welcome crunch.

MAKES 6 SERVINGS   **MEDIUM CROCKERY POT**

Combine the broth, rice, soy sauce, water chestnuts, bamboo shoots, Szechuan seasoning, and garlic in the crockery pot. Cover and cook on LOW until the rice is tender and the liquid has been absorbed, 3 to 4 hours.

PER SERVING: 153 calories, 1.1 g fat, 122 mg sodium, 2.7 g dietary fiber.

QUICK TIPS: Other spice blends that are excellent in this dish include Thai and Cajun seasonings.

Stuffed Pasta Shells with Mushroom Sauce

8 ounces (228 g) mushrooms, sliced

2 teaspoons olive oil

2 soy-sausage breakfast patties (or
   regular breakfast sausage)

1 can (28 ounces, 800 g) plum tomatoes,
   cut up

1 can (6 ounces, 170 g) low-sodium
   tomato paste

½ teaspoon dried oregano

½ teaspoon garlic powder

½ cup (120 ml) dry white wine

1 package (20 ounces, 570 g) low-fat
   cheese-stuffed pasta shells

Snipped fresh Italian parsley,
   for garnish

Store-bought shells minimize preparation time. The hearty sauce is rich with mushroom flavor.

MAKES 6 SERVINGS   **LARGE CROCKERY POT**

Sauté the mushrooms in the oil in a nonstick skillet until golden, about 5 minutes. Transfer them to the crockery pot.

In the same skillet, cook the sausage patties for 6 minutes. Remove them from the skillet, and cut them into ¼-inch (6 mm) cubes. Place the pieces in the crockery pot.

Stir in the tomatoes, tomato paste, oregano, garlic, and wine. Cover and cook on HIGH for 3½ to 5 hours.

Add the shells to the sauce, making certain to cover them with sauce. Cover and cook until the shells are thoroughly hot, about 1 hour. Garnish with the parsley.

PER SERVING: About 212 calories, 6.9 g fat (28% of calories), 1.9 g saturated fat, 8.3 mg cholesterol, 584 mg sodium, 3.4 g dietary fiber.

COOK'S NOTE: For a quick buffet dish, double the recipe and use either the stuffed shells or ravioli.

Savory Turnip Bowls with Bacon and Onions

½ cup (120 ml) low-sodium
    vegetable broth

2 large white turnips, (12 ounces, 341 g,
    each), scrubbed

1 medium potato, quartered

1 small onion, quartered

1 tablespoon snipped fresh dill or
    1 teaspoon dried dillweed

2 slices crisp bacon, crumbled

⅛ teaspoon freshly ground
    black pepper

Here's a clever turnip presentation that's company-special yet everyday easy.

MAKES 2 SERVINGS   **MEDIUM RECTANGULAR CROCKERY POT**

Pour the broth into the crockery pot. Slice a thin piece from the bottom of each turnip so the turnips sit flat. Using a melon baller, scoop out the interior of each turnip, leaving a ¼-inch (6 mm) shell and reserving the interior. Place the shells in the crockery pot.

Shred the reserved turnip, potatoes, and onions in a food processor. Mix in the dill and bacon. Spoon the turnip mixture into the shells. Cover and cook on LOW until the turnip is tender, 3 to 5 hours. Sprinkle with the pepper.

PER SERVING: About 169 calories, 3.5 g fat (17% of calories), 1.2 g saturated fat, 5 mg cholesterol, 300 mg sodium, 1.6 g dietary fiber.

COOK'S NOTE: To cook 4 or more turnip bowls at once, use an electric skillet. Set the heat to simmer.

Harvest Potatoes

1 cup (240 ml) fat-free chicken broth

2 teaspoons pickling spice, tied in
    cheesecloth

4 large potatoes, peeled and cut into
    ½-inch (13 mm) cubes

2 cloves garlic, pressed

Snipped fresh chives, for garnish

Garlic and pickling spices give everyday potatoes a mellow, captivating flavor. Serve these taters with beef, pork, or lamb roasts.

MAKES 4 SERVINGS   **MEDIUM CROCKERY POT**

Pour the broth into the crockery pot, and place the spices in the center bottom of the crockery pot. Add the potatoes and garlic. Cover and cook on LOW for 5 to 6 hours. Garnish with the chives.

PER SERVING: About 69 calories, 0.3 g fat (4% of calories), 0 g saturated fat, 0 g cholesterol, 46 mg sodium, 1 g dietary fiber.

COOK'S NOTES: These potatoes are best when served fresh.

To make 4 servings, use small to medium potatoes.

If pickling spice isn't available, substitute a bay leaf and a teaspoon each of whole peppercorns and whole nutmeg. These may be placed in a mesh tea ball for cooking.

Curried Butternut Squash with Cilantro

¼ cup (60 ml) fat-free chicken broth

2 medium butternut squash, peeled and cut into 1-inch (2.5 cm) cubes

1 tablespoon curry powder

⅛ teaspoon freshly ground black pepper

4 sprigs of fresh cilantro, snipped

The distinctive and intriguing flavor of curry dominates in this fast-to-fix side dish. Serve with roast chicken or turkey.

MAKES 4 SERVINGS　　　　　　　**MEDIUM CROCKERY POT**

Pour the broth into the crockery pot. Toss the squash with the curry, and add it to the crockery pot. Cover and cook on LOW until the squash is tender, 6 to 8 hours. Transfer to a serving bowl and sprinkle with the pepper and cilantro.

PER SERVING: About 88 calories, 0.4 g fat (4% of calories), 0 g saturated fat, 0 mg cholesterol, 30 mg sodium, 4 g dietary fiber.

COOK'S NOTE: After 6 to 8 hours of cooking, the squash is very tender. For firmer squash, cook 4 to 5 hours.

Light Baked Beans

1 can (14 ounces, 400 g) diced tomatoes

1½ cups (342 g) rinsed and drained canned great northern beans

2 slices bacon, cooked and crumbled

1 onion, minced

½ teaspoon crushed garlic

¼ cup (170 g) molasses

1 tablespoon Dijon mustard

Looking for great-tasting beans in a spicy-sweet fresh sauce? End your quest. This recipe fills the bill, without the usual almost gluey texture. Bonus: These beans keep nicely in the refrigerator for 3 to 4 days, or in the freezer for up to 3 weeks.

MAKES 6 SERVINGS　　　　　　　**MEDIUM CROCKERY POT**

Combine the tomatoes with their juice, beans, bacon, onions, garlic, molasses, and mustard in the crockery pot. Cover and cook on LOW until the flavors are blended and the mixture is very hot, 4 to 5 hours.

PER SERVING: 126 calories, 1.7 g fat, 60 mg sodium, 4.2 g dietary fiber.

QUICK TIPS: For convenience, use crushed garlic from a jar, and use a mini-food processor to mince the onion.

Herbed Potatoes and Carrots

2 carrots, cut into ½-inch (13 mm) slices

2 medium potatoes, cut into ½-inch (13 mm) cubes

4 large scallions, white part only, cut into ½-inch (13 mm) slices

¼ cup (60 ml) vegetable broth

Dash of freshly ground black pepper

Sprig of lemon thyme or ¼ teaspoon dried thyme leaves

The natural sweetness of carrots pairs perfectly with the tart flavor of lemon. This easy recipe uses the herb lemon thyme.

MAKES 4 SERVINGS   **MEDIUM CROCKERY POT**

Place the carrots, potatoes, and scallions in the crockery pot. Add the broth, pepper, and thyme. Cover and cook on HIGH until the vegetables are tender, 4 to 6 hours. Discard the lemon thyme.

PER SERVING: About 61 calories, 0.1 g fat (2% of calories), 0 g saturated fat, 0 mg cholesterol, 22 mg sodium, 1.9 g dietary fiber.

Tomatoes Stuffed with Beans and Rice

4 large tomatoes

½ cup (100 g) cooked long-grain rice, such as Basmati

1 small onion, chopped

½ green bell pepper, chopped

½ cup (114 g) fat-free refried beans

¼ cup (20 g) chopped fresh parsley

¼ teaspoon cumin seeds

½ teaspoon chili powder

½ teaspoon crushed red pepper flakes

¼ cup (60 ml) salsa with cheese

In this recipe, juicy ripe tomatoes serve as bowls for a satisfying, creamy filling of refried beans and rice. The flavors — cumin, chili, and peppers — are superbly Southwestern.

MAKES 4 SERVINGS   **MEDIUM CROCKERY POT**

Slice the tops off the tomatoes. Using a melon baller, scoop out the pulp and place it in a sieve. Using the back of a wooden spoon, press out the juice, discarding it, and chop the tomato pulp.

Combine 1 cup (200 g) of pulp (set the remaining pulp aside for another use), rice, onions, peppers, refried beans, parsley, cumin seeds, chili powder, and pepper flakes in a bowl. Spoon into the tomatoes.

Pour 2 tablespoons of water into the bottom of the crockery pot. Arrange the tomatoes, in 2 layers if necessary, in the crockery pot. Cover and cook on LOW until hot and flavorful, 3 to 4 hours.

PER SERVING: 155 calories, 2.4 g fat, 486 mg sodium, 5.5 g dietary fiber.

QUICK TIP: Leave the sides of the tomatoes about ¼- to ½-inch (7-13 mm) thick when removing the pulp; thick sides will help the tomatoes retain their shape during cooking.

HERBED POTATOES AND CARROTS

Garlic Mashed Potatoes

6 potatoes, peeled and quartered

8 cloves garlic, minced

1 tablespoon minced dried onions

2 cups (480 ml) water

Pinch of white pepper

¾ cups (180 ml) milk

Garlicky spuds like these are a hot item in many trendy restaurants. Fortunately, duplicating the flavor is satisfyingly simple.

MAKES 4 SERVINGS   **MEDIUM CROCKERY POT**

Combine potatoes, garlic, onions, and water in the crockery pot. Cover and cook on LOW or HIGH until the potatoes are very tender, 5 to 6 hours on LOW or 3 to 4 hours on HIGH.

Drain and remove the potatoes to a bowl. Using a potato masher, mash the potatoes with pepper and milk; finish by whipping them with an electric mixer, if desired.

PER SERVING: 203 calories, 0.3 g fat (1% of calories), 0.1 g saturated fat, 1 mg cholesterol, 39 mg sodium, 3.9 g dietary fiber.

QUICK TIP: Too rushed to peel and chop eight cloves of garlic? Use 4 teaspoons minced garlic from a jar instead.

Pasta Shells and Sauce with Chickpeas

1 can (28 ounces, 800g) crushed tomatoes

1 can (19 ounces, 540 g) chickpeas, rinsed and drained

6 cloves garlic, minced

1 teaspoon sugar

1 teaspoon Italian herb seasoning

1 tablespoon red wine vinegar

4 slices dried eggplant, finely chopped (optional)

6 fresh basil leaves, finely snipped

12 ounces (340 g) medium pasta shells

2 tablespoons grated Parmesan cheese

Saucy but simple, this version of traditional Italian pasta and beans goes together in minutes. Enjoy it with a crisp salad and a glass of red wine.

MAKES 4 SERVINGS   **MEDIUM CROCKERY POT**

Combine the tomatoes, chickpeas, garlic, sugar, seasoning, vinegar, and eggplant (if you wish to use eggplant) in the crockery pot. Cover and cook on LOW for 6 to 8 hours to make the sauce. During the last hour, cook the shells separately and drain them; keep warm. Stir the basil into the sauce and serve it over the pasta. Top each serving with the cheese.

PER SERVING: About 444 calories, 3.8 g fat (8% of calories), 0.5 g saturated fat, 1.6 mg cholesterol, 382 mg sodium, 2.2 g dietary fiber.

Butternut Squash and Onion Puree

¾ cup (180 ml) fat-free chicken broth

1 onion, chopped

1 butternut squash, peeled and cut into
    1-inch (2.5 cm) cubes

2 medium potatoes, peeled and cut into
    1-inch (2.5 cm) cubes

Freshly ground black pepper

This unique pairing is just what the veggie meister ordered: a golden, palate-friendly dish that's as easy as 1-2-3.

MAKES 4 SERVINGS　　　　　　　　**MEDIUM CROCKERY POT**

Combine the broth, onions, butternut squash, and potatoes in the crockery pot. Cover and cook on LOW or HIGH until the squash and potatoes are tender, 5 to 6 hours on LOW or 3 to 4 hours on HIGH.

Using a hand-held immersion blender or a potato masher, process the squash–onion mixture until smooth. Top each serving with the pepper.

PER SERVING: 155 calories, 1.3 g fat (7% of calories), 0.3 g saturated fat, 0 mg cholesterol, 39 mg sodium, 1.9 g dietary fiber.

Easy Orange-Glazed Carrots

1 cup (240 ml) water

1 package (16 ounces, 455 g)
    baby carrots

2 tablespoons orange juice

¼ cup (82 g) all-fruit orange
    marmalade spread

Pinch of ground nutmeg

Got a bit of a sweet tooth? Then these baby carrots coated with a sweet marmalade glaze could make your day. A pinch of nutmeg lends spicy warmth to the glaze.

MAKES 4 SERVINGS　　　　　　　　**MEDIUM CROCKERY POT**

Combine the water and carrots in the crockery pot. Cover and cook on LOW or HIGH until the carrots are tender, 5 to 6 hours on LOW or 3 to 4 on HIGH. Combine the orange juice, marmalade, and nutmeg on a a small microwave-safe bowl. Microwave on medium until hot, 1 to 3 minutes.

Using a slotted spoon, remove the carrots to a serving bowl. Drizzle with the marmalade mixture, and toss to coat.

PER SERVING: 108 calories, 0.3 g fat (2% of calories), 0.1 g saturated fat, 0 mg cholesterol, 46 mg sodium, 4.4 g dietary fiber.

QUICK TIPS: For an even sweeter glaze, add 1 teaspoon brown sugar to the marmalade mixture.

Rosemary's Saucy Green Beans

1 pound (445 g) fresh green beans

1 can (28 ounces, 800 g) crushed
tomatoes

2 strips crisp bacon, crumbled

4 cloves garlic, minced

1 teaspoon dried rosemary

⅛ teaspoon freshly ground
black pepper

Believe it or not, these beans are crisp-tender even after simmering for hours. And their flavor? It's the greatest!

MAKES 8 SERVINGS　　　　　　**MEDIUM CROCKERY POT**

Combine the beans, tomatoes, bacon, garlic, rosemary, and pepper in the crockery pot. Cover and cook on LOW until the beans are tender, 5 to 7 hours.

PER SERVING: About 64 calories, 1 g fat (13% of calories), 0.3 g saturated fat, 1.3 mg cholesterol, 271 mg sodium, 2.7 g dietary fiber.

COOK'S NOTE: Though their flavor's not as intense, 2 tablespoons of store-bought bacon-flavored bits or 2 slices of minced Canadian bacon can replace the crumbled bacon.

Pecan-Rice Cabbage Packets

1 medium onion, chopped

¼ cup (50 g) long-grain white or
brown rice

¼ cup (20 g) snipped fresh parsley

¼ cup (25 g) finely chopped pecans

¼ cup (42 g) currants

1 can (6 ounces, 170 g) tomato paste

½ teaspoon sugar

¼ teaspoon ground allspice

¼ teaspoon paprika

4 large green cabbage leaves

1 cup (240 ml) fat-free chicken broth

1 cup (240 ml) water

Kitchen string

A symphony of fruity, nutty flavor simmers in these fast-to-fix bundles, each of which makes a complete meal. If currants and pecans aren't readily available, substitute raisins and walnuts.

MAKES 4 SERVINGS　　　　　　**LARGE CROCKERY POT**

Mix together the onions, rice, parsley, pecans, currants, tomato paste, sugar, allspice, and paprika for the filling. Remove the tough rib from each cabbage leaf. Divide the filling among the leaves, placing some in the center of each. Fold in the leaf edges, and fasten each packet together with the string. Place the packets in the crockery pot.

Combine the chicken broth and water; pour it over the cabbage packets. Cover and cook on HIGH for 4 to 6 hours.

PER SERVING: About 195 calories, 5.7 g fat (25% of calories), 0.5 g saturated fat, 0 mg cholesterol, 126 mg sodium, 4.1 g dietary fiber.

COOK'S NOTE: To make tightly rolled packets, first blanch the cabbage leaves for 3 to 5 minutes and cool them; then add the filling. Finish cooking as per the recipe.

ROSEMARY'S SAUCY GREEN BEANS

Zin Cranberries

2 packages (12 ounces, 340 g, each)
    fresh cranberries

3 cups (600 g) sugar

2 cups (480 ml) California
    Zinfandel wine

1 cinnamon stick

2 teaspoons grated orange peel

2 oranges, segments cut into
    ½-inch (13 mm) pieces

½ cup (85 g) currants

Fruity and sweet, zin cranberries garner rave reviews from holiday dinner guests. Serve with turkey and pork roasts.

YIELDS ABOUT 7 CUPS (1.65 L)   **LARGE CROCKERY POT**

Mix the cranberries, sugar, Zinfandel, cinnamon, orange peel, and orange segments in the crockery pot. Cover and cook on HIGH until at least half of the cranberries pop, 5 to 7 hours. Remove the cinnamon stick, and stir in the currants. Cool to room temperature, then chill.

PER ½ CUP (120 ML): About 245 calories, 0.2 g fat (1% of calories), 0 g saturated fat, 0 mg cholesterol, 24 mg sodium, 2.9 g dietary fiber.

COOK'S NOTE: Refrigerated in a covered container, the cranberries will keep for up to 3 weeks.

Pureed Sweet Potatoes

4 sweet potatoes, peeled and cut into
    ¾-inch (20 mm) pieces

¾ cup (180 ml) orange juice

1 teaspoon grated orange peel

Pinch of white pepper

This orange and sweet potato dish is simple and superb tasting— everything it should be. Why not give it a try tonight?

MAKES 4 SERVINGS   **MEDIUM CROCKERY POT**

Combine potatoes and orange juice in the crockery pot. Cover and cook on LOW or HIGH until the potatoes are very tender, 5 to 6 hours on LOW or 3 to 4 hours on HIGH.

Using a potato masher or a hand-held immersion blender, process the mixture until smooth. Stir in the orange peel and pepper.

PER SERVING: 231 calories, 4.7 g fat (17% of calories), 0.8 g saturated fat, 0 mg cholesterol, 106 mg sodium, 3.9 g dietary fiber.

QUICK TIP: When grating orange peel, use the colored part, which is on the surface, only. The white part, or pith, tastes bitter.

Maple-Candied Sweet Potatoes

¼ cup (87 g) maple syrup

¼ cups (60 ml) apple juice

1 tablespoon butter

4 small sweet potatoes, peeled

½ cup (80 g) raisins

Raisins and maple syrup bring out the natural sweetness of these golden potatoes. Serve them often; they're a snap to fix.

MAKES 4 SERVINGS   **MEDIUM CROCKERY POT**

Mix the syrup and juice in the crockery pot. Add the butter, potatoes, and raisins. Cover and cook on LOW until the potatoes are tender, 8 to 10 hours. Serve with the syrup from the crockery pot and raisins spooned over the potatoes.

PER SERVING: About 253 calories, 3.1 g fat (11% of calories), 1.9 g saturated fat, 8 mg cholesterol, 45 mg sodium, 4.2 g dietary fiber.

Spaghetti Squash Steamed with Peppercorns

2 cups (480 ml) water

1 tablespoon assorted peppercorns

1 spaghetti squash (3 pounds, 1.3 kg)

Picante Lentil Sauce or Simmered Spaghetti Sauce

Grated Parmesan cheese for topping

Slowly simmer spaghetti squash until it's al dente, and make one of the sauces in this book to go with it.

MAKES 4 SERVINGS   **LARGE RECTANGULAR CROCKERY POT**

Place the water and peppercorns in the crockery pot. Using a sturdy two-pronged fork or a paring knife, pierce the shell of the squash in numerous places so it doesn't explode. Place it in the crockery pot. Cover and cook on LOW until the squash is tender, 7 to 9 hours. Serve topped with sauce and grated Parmesan cheese.

PER SERVING: About 31 calories, 0.1 g fat (3% of calories), 0.1 g saturated fat, 0 mg cholesterol, 5 mg sodium, 2.2 g dietary fiber.

Popular Poultry Entrées

Herbed Italian Chicken

½ cup (120 ml) dry white wine

1 tablespoon balsamic vinegar

1 pound (455 g) boneless, skinless chicken breasts, cut into 4 pieces

2 teaspoons olive oil

4 cloves garlic, chopped

¼ teaspoon crushed red pepper flakes

1 teaspoon Italian herb seasoning

⅛ teaspoon white pepper

4 ounces (115 g) white mushrooms, sliced, or 2 portobello mushrooms, diced

2 shallots, sliced

4 plum tomatoes, sliced

2 tablespoons seasoned dry bread crumbs

Snipped fresh parsley, for garnish

This Italian-inspired chicken-and-mushroom entrée rates A-1 for flavor and ease of preparation. It can also be the basis of Chicken Parmigiana. Serve it with mashed potatoes and a simple salad.

MAKES 4 SERVINGS　　　　　　　**MEDIUM CROCKERY POT**

Pour the wine and vinegar into the crockery pot. In a skillet over medium-high heat, brown the chicken on all sides in 1 teaspoon of the oil, for about 5 minutes. Transfer the chicken to the crockery pot, and sprinkle each piece with the garlic and pepper flakes, herb seasoning, and white pepper.

In the same skillet, sauté the mushrooms in the remaining oil until golden, about 4 minutes. Spoon them over the chicken. Top everything with the shallots. Cover and cook on LOW until the chicken is tender, 7 to 9 hours.

Transfer the chicken and toppings to a broiler-safe pan; top the chicken with the tomatoes and the crumbs. Broil until the crumbs are golden, about 1 minute, and garnish with the parsley.

PER SERVING: About 279 calories, 5.7 g fat (19% of calories), 1.4 g saturated fat, 96 mg cholesterol, 119 mg sodium, 1.3 g dietary fiber.

COOK'S NOTE: For **CHICKEN PARMIGIANA**, grate 4 ounces (115 g) of part skim milk mozzarella cheese and 2 ounces (56 g) of Parmesan cheese. Top the chicken, tomato, and bread-crumb mixture with the shredded mozzarella and Parmesan cheeses. Broil until the cheese is melted and has just started to brown.

Turkey Cutlets and Pasta with Black Olives

1 pound (455 g) turkey cutlets, cut into 1- x 3-inch (2.5 x 7.5 cm) pieces

1 teaspoon olive oil

1 medium onion, finely chopped

¼ cup (27 g) canned chopped roasted sweet peppers

4 cloves garlic, minced

½ cup (120 ml) fat-free chicken broth

2 tablespoons dry sherry

½ teaspoon Louisiana hot sauce

¼ teaspoon dried thyme leaves

¼ cup (60 ml) evaporated skim milk

¼ cup (21 g) grated Parmesan cheese

8 ounces (228 g) ziti or rotini

8 black olives, sliced

Cheese, olives and turkey form a tasty trio in this easy-to-make entrée. Serve with a mixed green salad or hot steamed peas.

MAKES 4 SERVINGS　　　　　　　**MEDIUM CROCKERY POT**

Brown the turkey in the oil in a skillet over medium-high heat, 3 to 5 minutes. Transfer to an electric crockery pot. Add the onions, peppers, garlic, broth, sherry, hot sauce, and thyme. Cover and cook on LOW until the turkey is cooked through and tender, 6 to 8 hours. In the last half-hour, cook the pasta separately; drain and keep warm.

Meanwhile, stir the milk and cheese into the turkey mixture. Cook until the mixture is hot, 15 to 30 minutes. Serve it over the pasta and top with the olives.

PER SERVING: About 503 calories, 6.6 g fat (12% of calories), 1.9 g saturated fat, 100 mg cholesterol, 387 mg sodium, 3.9 g dietary fiber.

COOK'S NOTE: Low-fat (1%) milk may be substituted for the evaporated skim milk.

Creamy Chicken with Roasted Peppers

2 teaspoons olive oil

¾ pound (340 g) chicken, cut into ¾-inch (20 mm) pieces

1 onion, chopped

2 ribs celery, thinly sliced

4 ounces (113 g) portobello mushrooms, chopped

¾ cup (80 g) chopped roasted red peppers

1 can (10 ounces, 300 ml) reduced-fat cream of celery soup

¼ cup (60 ml) dry white wine

¾ cup (180 ml) fat-free milk

4 English muffins, split and toasted, or "bake and fill" puff pastry shells

Here's an updated fast and flavorful version of chicken à la king. If you like, you can stir in ½ cup (74 g) fresh or frozen peas shortly before cooking is done.

MAKES 4 SERVINGS　　　　　　　　**MEDIUM CROCKERY POT**

Heat the oil in a large skillet over medium-high heat. Add the chicken, onions, celery, and mushrooms. Cook, stirring occasionally, just until the chicken is lightly browned, about 10 minutes.

Combine the chicken mixture, red peppers, soup (undiluted), and wine in the crockery pot. Cover and cook on LOW until the chicken is cooked through and the flavors are blended, 6 to 8 hours. Stir in the milk and cook until heated through, 10 to 15 minutes.

Serve immediately over the muffins or in the shells.

PER SERVING: 383 calories, 8 g fat, 613 mg sodium, 5.1 g dietary fiber.

QUICK TIPS: Portobello mushrooms are firmer and meatier than white button mushrooms, but if you can't find the portobello variety, select and slice the button variety. Use store-bought roasted red peppers in a jar to save time.

Chicken with Spicy Noodles

1 pound (455 g) boneless skinless chicken breast, cut into ¾-inch (20 mm) pieces

1 cup (240 ml) fat-free chicken broth

4 cloves garlic, minced

1 red bell pepper, very thinly sliced

1¼ cups (100 g) sliced scallions

1 tablespoon minced gingerroot

½ teaspoon crushed red pepper flakes

2 tablespoons reduced-fat peanut butter

1 tablespoon reduced-sodium soy sauce

10 ounces (284 g) angel-hair pasta

2 tablespoons chopped unsalted peanuts

2 tablespoons snipped fresh parsley

Treat your taste buds to hot pepper zest and peanut crunch with this Szechuan-inspired dinner.

MAKES 4 SERVINGS　　　　　　　　**MEDIUM CROCKERY POT**

Combine the chicken, broth, and garlic in the crockery pot. Cover and cook on LOW until the chicken is cooked through and the flavors are blended, 6 to 8 hours. Stir in the bell pepper, scallions, gingerroot, and pepper flakes. Cover and cook for 10 minutes.

Combine the peanut butter and soy sauce in a small bowl. Heat on low in a microwave oven until the peanut butter has melted, about 40 seconds. and stir into the chicken–vegetable mixture. Heat for 5 minutes.

Meanwhile, cook the noodles according to package directions. Drain well and divide among 4 plates. Serve topped with the chicken, peanuts, and parsley.

PER SERVING: 511 calories, 9.6 g fat (17% of calories), 2 g saturated fat, 71 mg cholesterol, 265 mg sodium, 3.3 g dietary fiber.

QUICK TIP: Can't find any angel-hair pasta? Pick up some vermicelli or spaghettini instead.

Chicken Athenos

Juice of 1 lemon

2 cinnamon sticks

4 cloves garlic, minced

1 can (16 ounces, 455 g) cut tomatoes with basil

1 bay leaf

⅛ teaspoon black pepper

¼ cup (60 ml) dry sherry

1 onion, chopped

1 pound (455 g) boneless, skinless chicken breasts, trimmed of fat and cut into 4 pieces

1 teaspoon olive oil

¼ cup (28 g) crumbled feta cheese

8 ounces (228 g) broad noodles

Sprigs of fresh mint, for garnish

A delightful Greek-inspired dish that's infused with cinnamon and lemon and topped with feta cheese. Serve with a favorite taverna salad.

MAKES 4 SERVINGS　　　　　　　　**MEDIUM CROCKERY POT**

Combine the lemon juice, cinnamon, garlic, tomatoes, bay leaf, pepper, sherry, and onions in the crockery pot.

Brown the chicken on both sides in the oil in a nonstick skillet over medium-high heat, 2 to 4 minutes. Transfer the chicken to the crockery pot. Cover and cook on LOW for 8 to 10 hours. Discard the bay leaf. In the last half-hour, cook the noodles separately; drain and keep warm. Serve topped with chicken.

PER SERVING: About 374 calories, 8.4 g fat (20% of calories), 2.6 g saturated fat, 119 mg cholesterol, 610 mg sodium, 3.6 g dietary fiber.

COOK'S NOTE: Since the time of Greek mythology, mint has been a symbol of hospitality. For a flavor twist fit for the gods, garnish this dish with a few fresh mint sprigs.

Orange–Basil Chicken with Fruit Salsa

1 chicken breast (about 3 pounds, 1.36 kg)

1 orange, thinly sliced

12 fresh basil leaves

1 cup (240 ml) fat-free chicken broth

1 orange, sectioned and diced

1 pear, diced

1 shallot, thinly sliced

1 teaspoon olive oil

1 tablespoon cider vinegar

Dash of ground red pepper

1 teaspoon dry sherry

For sensational, refreshing flavor, you can't beat this fruit-and-poultry entrée. If perfect pears aren't available, substitute a red- or green-skinned apple in the salsa. This recipe will charm its way onto your menu often, guaranteed.

MAKES 4 SERVINGS   **MEDIUM CROCKERY POT**

Lift the chicken's skin and slide the orange slices and 10 basil leaves under it. Coat a large nonstick skillet with cooking spray and heat over high heat. Add the chicken and cook until nicely browned, turning occasionally, 10 to 12 minutes. Place in the crockery pot. Pour ½ cup (120 ml) of the broth into the same skillet and cook, stirring and scraping, for 2 minutes to deglaze the skillet. Pour into the crockery pot and add the remaining ½ cup (120 ml) broth. Cover and cook on LOW until the chicken is cooked throughout, its juices run clear, and a meat thermometer registers 170°F, 7 to 9 hours.

Meanwhile, mince the remaining 2 basil leaves. In a small bowl, combine the diced orange, pear, shallot, oil, vinegar, red pepper, sherry, and minced basil. Cover and refrigerate until ready to serve.

Divide the chicken into thirds. Freeze two-thirds for later use. Slice the remaining chicken, discarding the skin, oranges, and basil. Serve immediately with the orange–pear mixture.

PER SERVING: 274 calories, 5.4 g fat, 128 mg sodium, 2.6 g dietary fiber.

QUICK TIP: The technique of sliding seasonings under poultry skin also works well for whole chickens, turkeys, and Cornish hens.

Turkey Slices with Favorite Fruit

1 pound (455 g) turkey breast slices

1 teaspoon olive oil

2 shallots, thinly sliced

½ cup dried apples (28 g) or peaches (46 g)

½ cup (85 g) currants or golden raisins

⅛ teaspoon freshly ground black pepper

¼ cup (60 ml) water

Juice of 1 lemon

1 lemon thyme sprig or ½ teaspoon dried thyme

2 lemons, thinly sliced

Turkey gets a not-too-sweet apple-and-currant sauce in this recipe.

MAKES 4 SERVINGS   **MEDIUM CROCKERY POT**

Brown the turkey on both sides in the oil in a nonstick skillet over medium-high heat, about 5 minutes. Transfer the turkey to the crockery pot. Add the shallots.

Mix the apples, currants, pepper, water, and juice in a small bowl. Pour the mixture over the turkey. Add the thyme and top with the lemon slices. Cover and cook on LOW until the turkey is done and the fruit is tender, 5 to 7 hours. Discard the thyme sprig.

PER SERVING: About 275 calories, 4.5 g fat (14% of calories), 0.7 g saturated fat, 95 mg cholesterol, 70 mg sodium, 2.3 g dietary fiber.

ORANGE–BASIL CHICKEN WITH FRUIT SALSA

Mandarin Chicken

¾ pound (340 g) boneless, skinless chicken breasts

1 tablespoon balsamic vinegar

1 can (14 ounces, 420 ml) fat-free chicken broth

1 onion, cut into thin wedges

1 teaspoon dried tarragon

1 can (11 ounces, 313 g) mandarin oranges, drained

1 tablespoon honey

1 tablespoon reduced-sodium soy sauce

4 tablespoons cornstarch

8 ounces (228 g) Chinese wheat noodles

¼ cup (60 ml) cold water

freshly ground black pepper, garnish

Sweet and colorful, oranges—the mandarin variety, to be specific—brighten chicken and noodles in this Asian-influenced main dish. And did you know that mandarin oranges and tangerines are close cousins?

MAKES 4 SERVINGS　　　　　　　　**MEDIUM CROCKERY POT**

Combine the chicken, vinegar, broth, and onions in the crockery pot. Cover and cook on LOW until the chicken is cooked through and the flavors are blended, 6 to 8 hours.

Remove the chicken to a platter, reserving the broth. Keep the chicken warm. Pour the broth into a saucepan and stir in the tarragon, oranges, honey, and soy sauce. Combine the cornstarch and water in a measuring cup. Stir into the broth mixture, and cook, stirring, over medium heat until the sauce has thickened.

Meanwhile, cook the noodles according to package directions. Drain well and divide among 4 plates. Top with the chicken and sauce. Garnish with the pepper.

PER SERVING: 464 calories, 4.6 g fat (9% of calories), 0.9 g saturated fat, 71 mg cholesterol, 317 mg sodium, 3.9 g dietary fiber.

QUICK TIP: To cut an onion into thin wedges, halve a peeled onion from stem to root end, then slice the halves vertically into wedges.

Curried Chicken over Rice

1 pound (455 g) boneless, skinless chicken breasts, trimmed of fat and cut into 1-inch (2.5 cm) cubes

4 medium onions, halved lengthwise and thinly sliced

4 cloves garlic, minced

1 tablespoon low-sodium soy sauce

1 teaspoon curry powder

2 teaspoons chili powder

1 teaspoon turmeric

1 teaspoon ginger powder

1 tablespoon peanut oil

⅓ cup (80 ml) water

1⅛ cups (225 g) rice

A blend of curry, cumin, turmeric, and ginger gives this dish its captivating Asian flavor and rich golden color. Serve with a side dish of steamed peas.

MAKES 4 SERVINGS　　　　　　　　**MEDIUM CROCKERY POT**

Mix the chicken, onions, garlic, soy sauce, curry, chili, turmeric, ginger, oil and water in the crockery pot. Cover and cook on LOW until the chicken is tender and cooked through, 7 to 9 hours. In the last half-hour, cook the rice separately; keep it warm. Serve the chicken over the hot rice.

PER SERVING: About 346 calories, 8 g fat (21% of calories), 1.8 g saturated fat, 96 mg cholesterol, 241 mg sodium, 2.6 g dietary fiber.

COOK'S NOTES: The cooked curried chicken mixture can be frozen for up to a month. To reheat it, thaw it in the refrigerator, then heat it until hot and bubbly throughout.

Freeze the rice separately for up to two months, and thaw it in the refrigerator as well. Add one or two tablespoons of water to the rice before warming it.

Chicken Stroganov

1 pound (455 g) boneless, skinless chicken breasts, cut into 1-inch (2.5 cm) cubes

4 teaspoons olive oil

2 medium onions, chopped

1½ cups (115 g) mushrooms, sliced

½ cup (120 ml) dry white wine

¼ teaspoon black pepper

1 teaspoon paprika

½ cup (120 g) nonfat sour cream

8 ounces (228 g) broad egg noodles

Paprika, for garnish

Named after Count Paul Stroganov, a 19th-century Russian diplomat, traditional stroganov is rich with butter, beef, and sour cream. This twenty-first-century version packs the same intriguing flavors but has far less fat and fewer calories.

MAKES 4 SERVINGS   **MEDIUM CROCKERY POT**

In a skillet over medium-high heat, brown the chicken on all sides in 2 teaspoons of the oil, about 5 minutes. Transfer the chicken to the crockery pot.

In the same skillet over medium-high heat, sauté the onions and mushrooms in the remaining oil until the onions are golden, 3 to 4 minutes. Transfer the onion mixture to the crockery pot. Pour in the wine, and sprinkle the onion mixture with the pepper and paprika. Cover and cook on LOW until the chicken is tender and cooked through, 7 to 9 hours. In the last half-hour of cooking, cook and drain the noodles separately; keep them warm.

Using a slotted spoon, transfer the chicken to a platter, leaving the onion mixture and liquid in the crockery pot. Keep the chicken warm. Stir the sour cream into the onion mixture. Serve the chicken over the hot noodles, top with the sour cream sauce, and garnish with the paprika.

PER SERVING: About 507 calories, 9.7 g fat (18% of calories), 1.9 g saturated fat, 96 mg cholesterol, 107 mg sodium, 2.9 g dietary fiber.

COOK'S NOTE: To cut uncooked chicken breasts quickly and easily, use kitchen shears.

Chinese Chicken with Vegetables

2 strips bacon

1 pound (455 g) boneless, skinless chicken breast, cut into 1-inch (2.5 cm) pieces

1 cup thinly sliced celery

1 medium potato, cut into ½-inch (13 mm) cubes

1 cup sliced scallions

1 can (8 ounces, 228 g) bamboo shoots

1½ teaspoons five-spice powder

½ cup (120 ml) water

1 tablespoon dry sherry

1 tablespoon low-sodium soy sauce

2 tablespoons cornstarch

1 teaspoon sugar

Subtly seasoned with five-spice powder, this recipe captures the essence of a Shanghai-style dish.

MAKES 4 SERVINGS **MEDIUM CROCKERY POT**

Cook the bacon in a skillet over medium heat until crumbly, about 5 minutes. Drain on paper towels, crumble, and transfer to the crockery pot.

Pour off all but 2 teaspoons of the bacon drippings, and add the chicken to the skillet. Brown the chicken on all sides; then transfer it to the crockery pot. Stir in the celery, potatoes, scallions, bamboo shoots, five-spice powder, ½ cup (120 ml) of the water, and the sherry and soy sauce. Cover and cook on LOW until the chicken is cooked through and tender, 6 to 8 hours. In a measuring cup, combine the cornstarch, remaining water, and sugar. Pour into the chicken mixture and cook until the liquid has thickened, about 3 minutes.

PER SERVING: About 280 calories, 5.9 g fat (19% of calories), 1.8 g saturated fat, 99 mg cholesterol, 360 mg sodium, 1.9 g dietary fiber.

COOK'S NOTES: Five-spice powder, a pungent blend of cinnamon, cloves, fennel seed, star anise, and szechuan peppercorns, is available in Asian markets and in most supermarkets. For added color, garnish with thin strips of sweet red pepper.

Mexican-Inspired Turkey with Pinto Beans

1 cup (228 g) rinsed and drained canned pinto beans

2 onions, cut into wedges

1 can (14 ounces, 400 g) diced tomatoes

1 cup (240 ml) fat-free beef broth

6 cloves garlic, minced

2 tablespoons chili powder

1 teaspoon ground cumin

1 teaspoon cocoa

½ teaspoon oregano

¾ pound (340 g) turkey breast slices, cut into thin 1-inch (2.5 cm) long strips

2 tablespoons snipped fresh cilantro

Mole, a dark, spicy Mexican sauce, was the inspiration for the seasoning combination in this stick-to-your-ribs main dish.

MAKES 4 SERVINGS **MEDIUM CROCKERY POT**

Combine the beans, onions, tomatoes (with liquid), broth, garlic, chili powder, cumin, cocoa, and oregano in the crockery pot.

Coat a nonstick skillet with cooking spray and heat over medium-high heat. Add the turkey, and cook, stirring occasionally it until it's lightly browned, 3 to 5 minutes. Remove to the crockery pot. Cover and cook on LOW until the turkey is cooked through and no longer pink and the flavors are blended, 5 to 7 hours.

Divide among 4 plates; top each serving with the cilantro.

PER SERVING: 259 calories, 1.7 g fat (6% of calories), 0.3 g saturated fat, 71 mg cholesterol, 114 mg sodium, 8.8 g dietary fiber.

QUICK TIP: Can't find cilantro, which is sometimes called fresh coriander? Then go for fresh parsley.

CHINESE CHICKEN WITH VEGETABLES

Chicken with Cider Vinegar Sauce

1 teaspoon light margarine

⅔ cup (50 g) chopped shallots

1 tablespoon sugar

1 tablespoon cider vinegar

½ cup (120 g) fat-free chicken broth

1 pound (455 g) boneless, skinless chicken breasts, trimmed of fat, cut into 4 pieces and pounded to ⅛ inch (3 mm) thick

8 ounces (228 g) fresh spinach, stems removed

4 halves of canned apricots

1 tablespoon raisins

1 slice of sweet onion, quartered

¼ cup (313 g) drained canned mandarin oranges

Kitchen string

Butter-flavored nonstick spray

¼ cup (60 ml) cold water

2 tablespoons cornstarch

A simply delectable marriage of sweet and savory flavors. This elegant entrée—chicken breasts stuffed with spinach and apricots—takes about an hour to prepare.

MAKES 4 SERVINGS　　　　　　　　**MEDIUM CROCKERY POT**

Mix the margarine, shallots, sugar, vinegar, and broth in the crockery pot.

Place the chicken on a work surface, and top each piece with 5 or 6 spinach leaves. Divide the apricots, raisins, onions, and oranges evenly among the chicken pieces. Roll up the chicken, starting at a narrow end and enclosing the fruit-vegetable filling. Tie each roll with the string.

Coat a nonstick skillet with butter-flavored nonstick spray and warm over medium-high heat. Add the chicken rolls and brown them on all sides, 2 to 4 minutes. Transfer the rolls to the crockery pot. Cover and cook on LOW until the chicken is tender, 6 to 8 hours. Transfer the rolls to a platter, leaving the shallots and liquid in the crockery pot. Keep the rolls warm.

Combine the water and cornstarch in a measuring cup. Stir the cornstarch mixture into the vinegar sauce, and cook on HIGH, stirring frequently, until the sauce thickens, 1 to 2 minutes. Serve the sauce over the rolls.

PER SERVING: About 300 calories, 6 g fat (18% of calories), 1.4 g saturated fat, 96 mg cholesterol, 157 mg sodium, 2 g dietary fiber.

COOK'S NOTE: These rolls can also be made with turkey breast slices.

Chicken with Oranges and Mushrooms

¼ teaspoon white pepper

1½ teaspoons paprika

1 tablespoon flour

1 pound (455 g) boneless, skinless
    chicken thighs

Butter-flavored nonstick spray

4 ounces (114 g) mushrooms, sliced

¼ cup chopped onions

¼ cup (43 g) sweet green pepper,
    chopped

½ cup (120 ml) orange juice

2 tablespoons dry sherry

1½ teaspoons brown sugar

1 small orange, sliced

The fragrant essence of orange commands attention in this superior sweet-and-sour entrée. Enjoy it with simple side dishes such as radicchio salad and parsley potatoes.

MAKES 4 SERVINGS   **MEDIUM CROCKERY POT**

Whisk together the flour, paprika, and pepper; sprinkle over both sides of the chicken pieces. Mist the pieces with the butter-flavored spray, and brown them in a nonstick skillet over medium-high heat, about 5 minutes. Transfer the chicken to the crockery pot.

Coat the same skillet with the nonstick spray, and sauté the mushrooms over medium-high heat until golden, 3 to 4 minutes. Transfer the mushrooms to the crockery pot. Add the onions and peppers.

In a measuring cup, mix the juice, sherry, and sugar. Pour over the chicken and vegetables. Top with the orange slices. Cover and cook on LOW until the chicken is tender and cooked through, 8 to 10 hours.

PER SERVING: About 334 calories, 13 g fat (35% of calories), 3.5 g saturated fat, 107 mg cholesterol, 190 mg sodium, 1.9 g dietary fiber.

COOK'S NOTE: For a meal with less fat and cholesterol, substitute chicken breasts for the thighs.

Easy Turkey Meatballs

1¼ pounds (570 g) ground turkey breast

½ cup (40 g) quick-cooking oats

1 egg white

2 tablespoons dried minced onions

¼ cup (20 g) minced fresh parsley

½ teaspoon ground nutmeg

¼ teaspoon freshly ground
    black pepper

1 teaspoon Worcestershire sauce

1 tablespoon olive oil

1 cup (240 ml) fat-free chicken broth

¼ cup (60 ml) dry white wine

¾ cup (180 g) nonfat sour cream

Treat yourself — and your family — to flavor-packed meatballs that are right at home over baked potatoes, wide noodles, rice, or pasta. Garnish with paprika and serve with a side of green peas or beans for a complete and satisfying dinner.

MAKES 6 SERVINGS   **MEDIUM CROCKERY POT**

Combine the turkey, oats, egg white, onions, parsley, nutmeg, pepper, and Worcestershire sauce in a large bowl. Mix thoroughly but gently. Shape into 30 walnut-size meatballs.

Heat the oil in a large nonstick skillet over medium-high heat. Add the meatballs and cook until browned on all sides, turning frequently, 8 to 10 minutes.

Combine the broth and wine in the crockery pot. Add the meatballs. Cover and cook on LOW until the meatballs are cooked through and the flavors have blended tender, 5 to 6 hours. Stir in the sour cream. Serve immediately.

PER SERVING: 226 calories, 3.5 g fat, 132 mg sodium, 1 g dietary fiber.

QUICK TIP: Form firm meatballs; loose ones will crumble during cooking.

Chicken Casserole with Swiss Cheese

2 teaspoons olive oil

¾ pound (340 g) chicken breast, cut into ¾-inch (20 mm) cubes

4 ounces (114 g) mushrooms, sliced

1 can (28 ounces (800 g)) crushed tomatoes

4 large cloves garlic, crushed

12 fresh basil leaves, minced

1 tablespoon dried minced onions

2 teaspoons sugar

⅛ teaspoon celery seeds

⅛ teaspoon freshly ground nutmeg

1 teaspoon mild Louisiana-style pepper sauce

3 ounces (85 g) reduced-fat Swiss cheese, cubed

¼ cup (35 g) seasoned bread crumbs, toasted

8 ounces (228 g) rotelle

This hearty, home-style dish features tomatoes, pasta, chicken, and cheese. For a complete meal, serve it with your favorite tossed greens salad and a fat-free frozen yogurt for dessert.

MAKES 6 SERVINGS　　　　　　　　　**MEDIUM CROCKERY POT**

Heat the oil in a large skillet over medium-high heat. Add the chicken and mushrooms; sauté, stirring, until the chicken is lightly browned, 5 to 8 minutes.

Combine the chicken mixture, tomatoes, garlic, basil, onions, sugar, celery seeds, nutmeg, and pepper sauce in the crockery pot. Cover and cook on LOW until the the chicken is cooked through, 6 to 8 hours. Stir in the cheese and cook until melted, about 20 minutes.

Meanwhile, cook and pasta according to package directions. Drain well and divide among 6 places. Top with the chicken-tomato mixture and bread crumbs.

PER SERVING: 365 calories, 6.5 g fat, 439 mg sodium, 3.6 g dietary fiber.

QUICK TIPS: For maximum flavor, grind your own nutmeg, using either a nutmeg grinder or a hand-held cheese grater. And to toast bread crumbs, place them in a small nonstick skillet and cook over medium heat, shaking the skillet frequently, until lightly browned, 5 to 10 minutes.

Balsamic-Seasoned Turkey and Sweet Potatoes

1 turkey breast (4½ pounds, 2 kg)

1 can (14 ounces, 420 ml) fat-free chicken broth

1 cup (240 ml) dry white wine

1 tablespoon balsamic vinegar

2 sprigs fresh lemon thyme

1 teaspoon olive oil

½ teaspoon lemon pepper

½ teaspoon fennel seeds

4 sweet potatoes

2 leeks, white part only, sliced

Enjoy a quick Thanksgiving-style dinner year-round. This humble meal of turkey and sweet potatoes goes together with little effort, so you can serve it often. A side of green peas or beans rounds out the meal nicely.

MAKES 6 SERVINGS　　　　　　　　　**LARGE CROCKERY POT**

Coat a large skillet with cooking spray and heat over high heat. Add the turkey and cook until browned on all sides. Let cool slightly.

Combine the broth, wine, vinegar, and lemon thyme in the crockery pot. Add the turkey. Rub the exposed area of the turkey with the oil; sprinkle with the lemon pepper and fennel. Arrange the potatoes and leeks around the turkey. Cover and cook on LOW until the turkey is tender; the juices run clear; and a meat thermometer, inserted in the thickest part of the breast, registers 170°F; and the potatoes are tender, 8 to 10 hours on LOW or 6 to 8 hours on HIGH.

Let rest for 10 minutes. Divide the turkey into 6 equal sections. Package and store 5 sections for future use. Slice the remaining part and serve with the potatoes and leeks.

PER SERVING: 295 calories, 4.1 g fat, 184 mg sodium, 3 g dietary fiber.

QUICK TIP: Leave the turkey skin in place during cooking to maintain juiciness, but remove it before serving to reduce calories and fat intake.

Turkey with Creole Seasoning

2¼ cups (540 ml) fat-free chicken broth

2 teaspoons paprika

1½ teaspoons garlic powder

1½ teaspoons freshly ground
  black pepper

1½ teaspoons dried minced onions

1½ teaspoons crushed red
  pepper flakes

¾ teaspoon dried thyme

¾ teaspoon white pepper

cooking spray

1 pound (455 g) boneless, skinless
  turkey breast

3 tablespoons *cold* water

2 tablespoons cornstarch

½ teaspoon browning and
  seasoning sauce

Spice rubs are hot! Use this one to add character to a succulent steamed turkey breast. The rub gets its fire from black, white, and red peppers.

MAKES 4 SERVINGS   **MEDIUM CROCKERY POT**

Pour the broth into the crockery pot.

In a small bowl, combine the paprika, garlic, black pepper, onions, red pepper, thyme, and white pepper. Coat a nonstick skillet with cooking spray and heat over high heat. Add the turkey and cook, turning occasionally, until browned on all sides. Let cool enough to handle. Rub the seasonings over the turkey. Place in the crockery pot. Cover and cook on LOW until the turkey is cooked through, the juices run clear, and a meat thermometer registers 170°F when inserted in the thickest part of the meat, 6 to 8 hours.

Remove to a platter, reserving the broth; keep the turkey warm.

Pour the broth into a saucepan. In a small cup, combine the water, cornstarch, and browning sauce. Pour into the broth and cook over medium heat until slightly thickened, about 3 minutes. Slice the turkey and serve it with the broth mixture.

PER SERVING: 203 calories, 1.1 g fat (5% of calories), 0.3 g saturated fat, 94 mg cholesterol, 162 mg sodium, 0.7 g dietary fiber.

QUICK TIP: If you're watching your sodium intake, be certain to select garlic powder, not garlic salt.

Chicken Parmesan

2 teaspoons olive oil

4 skinless, boneless chicken breasts
(about 3 ounces, 85 g, each)

1¼ cups (250 g) crushed tomatoes

2 large cloves garlic, crushed

1 teaspoon sugar

Pinch of celery seeds

2 tablespoons dry red wine

½ cup (55 g) shredded
mozzarella cheese

2 tablespoons grated Parmesan cheese

In this simple dish, the classic duo of tomatoes and cheese takes chicken from ordinary to extraordinary. Mark the recipe for future reference. It's so tasty, you'll have numerous requests to serve it often.

MAKES 4 SERVINGS   **MEDIUM CROCKERY POT**

Heat the oil in a nonstick skillet over medium-high heat. Add the chicken and sauté, stirring occasionally, until lightly browned, about 10 minutes.

Combine the chicken, tomatoes, garlic, sugar, celery seeds, and wine in the crockery pot. Cover and cook on LOW until the chicken is cooked through and a meat thermomter registers 170°F, 6 to 8 hours.

Combine the cheeses in a small bowl and sprinkle them over the chicken. Don't stir. Cook until the cheeses are melted, about 15 minutes.

PER SERVING: 249 calories, 8.3 g fat, 364 mg sodium, 1.3 g dietary fiber.

QUICK TIP: To save time, select store-bought shredded and grated cheeses; but to get maximum flavor, freshly shred and grate the cheeses.

Paprika Chicken in Wine

½ cup (120 ml) dry white wine

2 teaspoons olive oil

1 pound (455 g) boneless, skinless
chicken breasts, trimmed of fat
and cut into 4 pieces

1 teaspoon cumin seeds

1 teaspoon mustard seeds

4 cloves garlic, minced

1 tablespoon paprika

1 large onion, thinly sliced

4 ounces (114 g) mushrooms, sliced

Sprigs of parsley, for garnish

Sweet red pepper rings, for garnish

Whole spices and plenty of paprika impart a pleasantly intense flavor to this entrée. Serve with creamy mashed potatoes and a tomato and lettuce salad.

MAKES 4 SERVINGS   **LARGE CROCKERY POT**

Pour the wine into the crockery pot. Heat 1 teaspoon of the oil in a skillet, and brown the chicken on both sides over medium-high heat, 3 to 5 minutes. Transfer the chicken to the crockery pot, and sprinkle on the cumin, mustard, garlic, and paprika.

Add the remaining oil to the same skillet and sauté the onions and mushrooms until lightly browned, 2 to 3 minutes. Spoon over the chicken in the crockery pot. Cover and cook on LOW until the chicken is tender, 7 to 9 hours. Garnish with the parsley and peppers.

PER SERVING: About 268 calories, 7 g fat (24% of calories), 1.5 g saturated fat, 96 mg cholesterol, 89 mg sodium, 1.3 g dietary fiber.

COOK'S NOTE: To cook this dish in a medium crockery pot, cut the chicken into smaller pieces and put the seasonings between the layers.

CHICKEN PARMESAN

Caribbean Chicken with Parsnips

2 tablespoons olive oil

4 skinless chicken breasts (about 8 ounces, 227 g, each)

2 gloves garlic, minced

1 pound (455 g) parsnips, cut into julienne strips

1 pound (455 g) potatoes, sliced ¼-inch (6 mm) thick

1 can (14 ounces, 420 g) fat-free chicken broth

¼ cup (60 ml) dry white wine or vermouth

2 tablespoons sofrito seasoning

1 lime, thinly sliced

¼ cup (36 g) Masarepa® (or other white precooked cornmeal)

This fuss-free dish uses sofrito and lime to give chicken the customary flavors of Caribbean fare. Make your own sofrito — a flavorful concoction of onions, green peppers, garlic, and annatto — or buy ready-made.

MAKES 4 SERVINGS   **LARGE CROCKERY POT**

Heat the oil in a large nonstick skillet over medium-high heat. Add the chicken and garlic and sauté, stirring occasionally, until the chicken is lightly browned on all sides, about 10 minutes.

Place the parsnips and potaoes in the crockery pot. Add the chicken, breast side up, and garlic. Combine the broth, wine, and sofrito in a small bowl and pour over the chicken. Arrange the lime slices over the chicken. Cover and cook on LOW until the chicken is cooked through, a meat thermometer registers 170°F and the potatoes are tender, 7 to 9 hours.

Remove the chicken and vegetables to a platter, reserving the liquid. Cover the chicken and vegetables with foil to keep warm. Pour the cooking liquid into a saucepan over medium heat. Gradually add the Masarepa, stirring constantly and vigorously to prevent lumps, and cook until thickened. Serve over chicken and vegetables.

PER SERVING: 389 calories, 3.7 g fat, 351 mg sodium, 7.3 g dietary fiber.

QUICK TIP: Can't find precooked cornmeal at the supermarket? Substitute instant flour, which dissolves and thickens quickly.

Turkey with Cranberry–Currant Sauce

1 cup (240 ml) fat-free chicken broth

1 onion, chopped

½ cup (85 g) currants or raisins

nonstick spray

1 pound (455 g) turkey breast fillets

4 potatoes, peeled and quartered

½ cup (165 g) jellied cranberry sauce

1 teaspoon grated orange peel

1 orange, with sections cut into ½-inch (13 mm) pieces

The popular flavors of cranberries, oranges, and turkey team up in this delectable entrée.

MAKES 4 SERVINGS   **MEDIUM CROCKERY POT**

Combine the broth, onion and currante in the crockery pot.

Coat a nonstick skillet with the cooking spray, and heat over medium-high heat. Add the turkey, and sauté, turning once or twice until browned on both sides, about 5 minutes. Remove to the crockery pot. Add the potatoes. Cover and cook on LOW until the turkey is cooked through, the flavors are blended, and the potatoes are tender, 6 to 8 hours.

Remove the turkey and potatoes to a platter, reserving the broth and onions; keep the turkey and potatoes hot.

Pour the broth mixture into a saucepan and stir in the cranberry sauce, orange peel, and orange sections. Cook over medium heat until the cranberries have melted and the sauce is slightly thickened, 3 to 5 minutes. Serve over the turkey.

PER SERVING: *413 calories, 1.1 g fat (2% of calories), 0.3 g saturated fat, 94 mg cholesterol, 119 mg sodium, 5.7 g dietary fiber.*

QUICK TIP: *Turkey breast fillets are sometimes difficult to find. If you can't locate any, use breast slices instead.*

Fajitas with Cumin Seeds

½ pound (228 g) lean chip steak, cut into thin strips

¼ cup (60 ml) fat-free beef broth

2 medium onions, halved lengthwise and thinly sliced

1 medium sweet green or red pepper, thinly sliced

6 cloves garlic, minced

½ teaspoon cumin seeds

1 chili pepper, minced

½ cup (75 g) frozen corn

½ cup (114 g) cooked black beans

Juice of 1 lime

4 flour or corn tortillas (8-inch, 20 cm, diameter)

4 tablespoons nonfat sour cream

½ cup (120 ml) medium or hot salsa

Sprigs of cilantro, for garnish

A lime-and-pepper marinade gives traditional steak fajitas their flavor and tenderness. Here, slow cooking achieves the same mouth-watering results.

MAKES 4 FAJITAS   **MEDIUM CROCKERY POT**

Combine the steak, broth, onions, sweet pepper, garlic, cumin, chili pepper, corn, and beans in the crockery pot. Cover and cook on LOW until the steak is tender, 7 to 9 hours. Stir in half the lime juice.

Divide the steak mixture among the tortillas; then roll them up. Place them in a microwave-safe baking dish and sprinkle them with the remaining lime juice. Warm everything in a microwave oven on high for 1 minute. To warm in a regular oven, cover with foil and place in a preheated oven for 5 minutes at 325°F (163°C). Top with the sour cream and salsa, and garnish with the cilantro.

PER FAJITA: *About 377 calories, 9.3 g fat (22% of calories), 3.2 g saturated fat, 34 mg cholesterol, 378 mg sodium, 3 g dietary fiber.*

COOK'S NOTE: *Ground cumin is a perfectly acceptable replacement for cumin seeds. Use a little less, however.*

Pollo Cacciatore

¾ pound (340 g) boneless, skinless chicken breasts, cut into 8 pieces

⅓ cup (50 g) whole-wheat flour

4 teaspoons olive oil

2 large scallions, sliced

4 cloves garlic, minced

1 cup (115 g) quartered small white mushroom caps

1 green bell pepper, thinly sliced

1 can (28 ounces, 800 g) plum tomatoes, cut up, with liquid

½ cup (120 ml) light Italian red wine

¼ teaspoon ground celery seeds

½ teaspoon Italian herb seasoning

¼ teaspoon freshly ground black pepper

Cacciatore lovers take note: This hunter-style stew is full to the brim with tender chicken, garlic, tomatoes, red wine, mushrooms and other ingredients that make Mediterranean foods so decidedly magnifico. Serve over mafalda or rotini, and top everything with snipped fresh Italian parsley and sliced green olives.

MAKES 4 SERVINGS　　　　　　　　**MEDIUM CROCKERY POT**

Coat the chicken with the flour. Heat 2 teaspoons of the oil in a nonstick skillet over medium-high heat. Add the chicken, and cook until lightly browned, about 5 minutes. Remove to the crockery pot.

In the same skillet, heat the remaining oil. Add the scallions, garlic, pepper, and mushrooms and sauté until the scallions are translucent, about 3 minutes. Remove to the crockery pot and stir in the tomatoes (with liquid), wine, celery seeds, Italian seasoning and black pepper. Cover and cook on LOW until the chicken is tender and cooked through, 6 to 8 hours.

PER SERVING: 291 calories, 8.5 g fat (26% of calories), 1.6 g saturated fat, 71 mg cholesterol, 84 mg sodium, 4.1 g dietary fiber.

QUICK TIP: Though you can use a domestic Italian-style wine in this recipe, you might want to try an imported Valpolicella or Bardolino.

Turkey in White Wine Sauce

½ cup (120 ml) dry white wine

¾ cup (180 ml) fat-free chicken broth

cooking spray

4 slices Canadian-style bacon

1 package (10 ounces, 284 g) frozen pearl onions, thawed

4 ounces (114 g) small mushroom caps

4 boneless skinless turkey breast slices (about 1 pound, 455 g)

1 tablespoon cornstarch

¼ teaspoon freshly ground black pepper

½ teaspoon dried thyme leaves

⅛ teaspoon ground celery seeds

8 ounces (228 g) broad noodles

Use any pleasant-tasting dry white wine in this sauce. So long as the wine is dry, not sweet, it'll impart the right delightful nuance.

MAKES: 4 SERVINGS　　　　　　　　**MEDIUM CROCKERY POT**

Pour the wine and ½ cup (120 ml) broth into the crockery pot.

Coat a nonstick skillet with the cooking spray, and heat over medium-high heat. Add the bacon and cook, turning, until lightly brown on both sides, about 3 minutes. Remove to the crockery pot. Stir in the onions.

Coat the same skillet with nonstick spray, and heat over high heat. Add the mushrooms and turkey. Cook until the mushrooms and turkey are brown, about 5 minutes. Remove turkey to the crockery pot. Cover and cook on LOW until the turkey is cooked through and the flavors are blended, 6 to 8 hours.

Remove the turkey and bacon to a platter, reserving the vegetables and broth; keep the turkey warm.

Pour the vegetables and broth into a saucepan. In a measuring cup, whisk together the cornstarch, pepper, thyme, celery seeds and the remaining ¼ cup (60 ml) broth. Stir into the vegetable–broth mixture. Cook until thickened and hot, about 2 minutes.

Meanwhile, cook the noodles according to the package directions. Drain well and serve topped with the turkey, bacon, and broth mixture.

PER SERVING: 447 calories, 2.5 g fat (5% of calories), 0.7 g saturated fat, 102 mg cholesterol, 291 mg sodium, 3.1 g dietary fiber.

QUICK TIP: To wash mushrooms, wipe them with a damp cloth or quickly rinse them under cool running water. Never soak mushrooms; they become waterlogged easily.

Savory Turkey Meatballs in Italian Sauce

1 can (28 ounces, 800 g) crushed tomatoes

1 tablespoon red wine vinegar

1 medium onion, finely chopped

2 cloves garlic, minced

¼ teaspoon Italian herb seasoning

1 teaspoon dried basil

1 pound (455 g) ground turkey breast

2 egg whites

⅛ teaspoon garlic powder

¼ teaspoon dried minced onion

⅛ teaspoon black pepper

⅓ cup (27 g) quick oats

⅓ cup (27 g) dried parsley

¼ cup (21 g) grated Parmesan cheese

¼ cup (35 g) unbleached flour

Nonstick spray

Seasoned just right with garlic, onion, and cheese, these meatballs have the taste of those grandmom used to make, but only a fraction of the fat. Enjoy them with spaghetti or in a hoagie roll.

MAKES 8 SERVINGS   **LARGE CROCKERY POT**

Combine the tomatoes, vinegar, onions, garlic, seasoning, and basil in the crockery pot. Cover and turn crockery pot on to LOW. In a bowl, mix the turkey, egg whites, garlic powder, dried onions, pepper, oats, parsley, and cheese. Form into 16 one-inch balls, and dredge each ball in the flour. Lightly mist the balls with the nonstick spray and brown them on all sides in a nonstick skillet over medium-high heat. Transfer them to the crockery pot. Cover and cook on LOW for 8 to 10 hours.

PER SERVING: About 183 calories, 2.2 g fat (11% of calories), 0.9 g saturated fat, 50 mg cholesterol, 349 mg sodium, 2.8 g dietary fiber.

COOK'S NOTES: These keep nicely in the freezer for up to a month.

AMERICAN PAELLA

American Paella

2⅓ cups (560 ml) fat-free chicken broth

1½ large red onions, coarsely chopped

3 cloves garlic, finely chopped

½ pound (228 g) boneless, skinless chicken breasts, cut into 1-inch (2.5 cm) cubes

1 jar (4 ounces (114 g)) roasted peppers, drained

1 teaspoon turmeric

½ teaspoon dried thyme leaves

⅛ teaspoon black pepper

⅓ cup (65 g) wild rice

1 cup (200 g) long-grain brown rice

½ pound (228 g) shrimp, shelled and deveined

1 cup (150 g) frozen peas

Wild rice makes classic Spanish paella an American main course. Complete this delicious one-dish meal with a favorite dessert.

MAKES 6 SERVINGS   **LARGE CROCKERY POT**

Combine the broth, onions, garlic, chicken, roasted peppers, turmeric, thyme, and black pepper in the crockery pot. Cover and cook on HIGH for 3 to 5 hours.

Stir in the shrimp and wild and brown rices. Cover and cook until the shrimp and rices are tender and most of the liquid has been absorbed, about 1¼ to 2 hours. Add more water while the rice is cooking, if needed. Stir in the peas and cook until they're tender, about 15 minutes.

PER SERVING: About 349 calories, 3.8 g fat (10% of calories), 0.7 g saturated fat, 89 mg cholesterol, 190 mg sodium, 5.7 g dietary fiber.

Turkey Tenders with Caper–Madeira Sauce

¼ cup (60 ml) vegetable broth

1 onion, finely chopped

1 pound (455 g) turkey tenders

1 tablespoon snipped fresh parsley

1 teaspoon capers, rinsed and drained

2 teaspoons Madeira

Looking for an uncommon entrée with fuss-free preparation? Then give this one a shot. The pairing of capers, small, sun-dried flower buds, and Madeira, a fortified Portuguese wine, results in a sauce of complex flavors and subtle richness. The dish is suitable for company but goes together with week-night ease.

MAKES 4 SERVINGS   **MEDIUM CROCKERY POT**

Combine the broth and the onion in the crockery pot. Arrange the turkey in the bottom of the pot. Cover and cook on LOW until the turkey is cooked through and a meat thermometer registers 170°F, 6 to 8 hours.

Remove the turkey to a platter and cover with foil to keep warm. Stir the parsley, capers, and Madeira into the liquid remaining in the pot. Slice turkey and spoon the Madeira sauce over the slices. Serve immediately.

PER SERVING: 174 calories, 0.9 g fat, 92 mg sodium, 0.7 g dietary fiber.

QUICK TIP: Capers are packed in a very salty brine. For best flavor, always rinse them before using.

Picadillo de Pavo

Nonstick spray

1 pound (445 g) ground turkey breast

1 large red onion, chopped

4 cloves garlic, minced

1 pound (445 g) plum tomatoes, thinly sliced

1 large green chili, chopped

1 teaspoon chili powder

1 teaspoon ground allspice

½ cup (160 g) raisins

8 flour tortillas

8 green stuffed olives, sliced, for garnish

Medium or hot salsa (optional)

Nonfat sour cream (optional)

Translated, this means turkey hash. Here, warm flour tortillas enclose a zesty combination of turkey, tomatoes, raisins, and seasonings for a family-pleasing, south-of-the-border-style dish.

MAKES 4 SERVINGS   **MEDIUM CROCKERY POT**

Coat a nonstick skillet with the nonstick spray. Cook the turkey in the skillet over medium-high heat, stirring frequently, until the meat is browned and crumbly, 4 to 5 minutes. Add the onions and garlic, and cook until the onions are translucent, 3 to 4 minutes. Transfer the mixture to the crockery pot.

Stir in the tomatoes, chili pepper, chili powder, allspice, and raisins. Cover and cook on LOW for 5 to 7 hours.

Divide the turkey mixture among the tortillas; garnish with the olive slices; serve with the optional salsa and sour cream.

PER SERVING: About 491 calories, 6.7 g fat (12% of calories), 1.1 g saturated fat, 95 mg cholesterol, 584 mg sodium, 2.9 g dietary fiber.

COOK'S NOTE: Corn tortillas make a tasty substitute for the wheat flour ones, and picante sauce can replace the salsa.

Glazed Turkey Breast Roast

2 bay leaves

1 teaspoon assorted peppercorns

Water to fill one inch (2.5 cm) of crockery pot

Nonstick cooking spray

3 cups (114 g) sourdough bread cubes

⅓ cup (00g) finely chopped Canadian bacon

1 medium onion, chopped

2 celery stalks, chopped

2 cloves garlic, minced

¼ cup (60 ml) fat-free chicken broth

¼ teaspoon white pepper

½ teaspoon sage

1½ pounds (675 g) boneless turkey breast

½ cup (165 g) currant, apricot or apple jelly

Not just for company: This tender, stuffed roast tastes as good as it looks! It's easy to prepare, too.

MAKES 6 SERVINGS   **LARGE CROCKERY POT (PLUS A COLLAPSIBLE VEGETABLE STEAMER BASKET)**

Place the bay leaves and peppercorns in the crockery pot. Add water to approximately 1 inch. Place a collapsible vegetable steamer basket in the crockery pot.

Coat a nonstick skillet with nonstick spray, and warm it over medium-high heat. Sauté the bread, bacon, onions, celery, and garlic until the onions are lightly browned, about 6 minutes. Stir in the white pepper and the sage. Transfer the bread stuffing to the steamer basket in the crockery pot.

Coat the same skillet with nonstick spray; rewarm over medium-high heat. Quickly brown the turkey breast on both sides; then transfer it to the crockery pot, placing it atop the stuffing.

Melt ¼ cup jelly and brush it on the turkey breast. Cover and cook on LOW until the breast is tender and cooked through, 190°F

(87.8°C) on a meat thermometer, 8 to 10 hours. Melt the remaining jelly and brush it on the breast.

PER SERVING: About 310 calories, 3 g fat (9% of calories), 0.9 g saturated fat, 104 mg cholesterol, 406 mg sodium, 1.3 g dietary fiber.

Chicken Picadillo

1 pound (445 g) boneless, skinless chicken breasts, cut into ½-inch (13 mm) cubes

2 large onions, chopped

8 cloves garlic, minced

1 can (15 ounces, 426 g) diced tomatoes

½ cup (80 g) raisins

1 red bell pepper, finely chopped

1 mild chili pepper, seeded and finely chopped

1 stick cinnamon

3 tablespoons instant flour

¼ teaspoon crushed red pepper flakes

6 black olives, sliced, optional

8 corn tortillas, warmed

"Picadillo" is Spanish for hash—plain and simple. Here, cubed chicken replaces the usual ground pork, and the hash is rolled up in a warm tortilla. Serve this super supper with salsa—medium or hot, depending on your palate's preference—and nonfat sour cream, if desired.

MAKES: 4 SERVINGS   **MEDIUM CROCKERY POT**

Heat a nonstick skillet over medium-high heat. Add the chicken, onions, and garlic, and cook, stirring occasionally, until the chicken is lightly browned, about 5 minutes. Remove to the crockery pot. Stir in the tomatoes, raisins, bell peppers, chili peppers, and cinnamon. Cover and cook on LOW until the chicken is cooked through and the flavors are blended, 6 to 8 hours.

Discard the cinnamon. Stir in the flour, red pepper flakes, and olives. Cook until the mixture has thickened, 5 to 10 minutes.

Spoon the hash down center of each tortilla. Roll up and serve.

PER SERVING: 474 calories, 6.8 g fat (12% of calories), 1.5 g saturated fat, 95 mg cholesterol, 239 mg sodium, 8 g dietary fiber.

QUICK TIP: To heat tortillas, wrap them in foil and bake in a 350° oven for 5 to 7 minutes.

Pork Chops Niagara

4 boneless center-cut loin pork chops, sliced ½ inch (13 mm) thick and trimmed of fat (about 1 pound, 455 g)

1 teaspoon olive oil

4 cloves garlic, crushed

½ teaspoon white pepper

1½ cups (360 ml) white wine (for example, New York State Niagara Grape)

2 shallots, thinly sliced

1 tomato, sliced

½ green bell pepper, thinly sliced in rings

4 potatoes, quartered

A New York state wine, with its characteristic subtle Concord grape flavor, makes this a deliciously different entrée. For a complete meal, accompany the dish with a light salad.

MAKES 4 SERVINGS　　　　　　　　　　**MEDIUM CROCKERY POT**

Rub the pork with the oil, garlic, and pepper.

Coat a nonstick skillet with cooking spray and heat over medium-high heat. Add the pork and cook until lightly browned on both sides, about 3 minutes a side. Remove to a crockery pot.

Pour half the wine into the skillet, and cook, stirring and scraping to deglaze the skillet, about 3 minutes. Pour into the crockery pot. Arrange the shallots, tomatoes, and bell peppers over the pork. Arrange the potatoes around the edges of the crockery pot. Pour in the remaining wine. Cover and cook on LOW or HIGH until the pork is cooked through, the potatoes are tender, and the flavors are blended, 5 to 6 hours on LOW or 3 to 4 hours on HIGH.

Serve the pork topped with the broth and vegetables.

PER SERVING: 384 calories, 8.6 g fat, 84 mg sodium, 3.1 g dietary fiber.

QUICK TIP: To deglaze the skillet, bring the wine to simmering and stir, loosening bits of browned food.

Mustard-Crusted Pot Roast with Potatoes

2¼ (540 ml) cups fat-free beef broth

2½-pound (1.14 kg) eye of round roast, trimmed of fat

¼ cup (60 ml) dry red wine

1 small onion, quartered

1 rib celery, quartered

1 small carrot, quartered

1 clove garlic, minced

1 bay leaf

1 teaspoon freshly ground black pepper

2 teaspoons black or yellow mustard seeds

6 potatoes, halved

Here's an updated pot roast with easy preparation and exceptional flavor. Mustard seeds and crushed peppercorns form a pleasing piquant crust; slow-cooking creates a tender roast. This recipe is top notch. Take my word for it!

MAKES 8 SERVINGS　　　　　　　　　　**MEDIUM CROCKERY POT**

Combine the broth, beef, wine, onion, celery, carrot, garlic, and bay leaf in a crockery pot. Press the pepper and mustard seeds into the beef above the liquid. Arrange the potatoes around the beef. Cover and cook on LOW until the beef is very tender and a meat thermometer registers at least 160°F or 71.1°C, 8 to 10 hours.

Remove the beef and potatoes to a serving platter, reserving the liquid. Discard the onion, carrot, celery and bay leaf. Slice the beef and serve with the potatoes and reserved cooking liquid.

PER SERVING: 348.9 calories, 7.4 g fat, 146 mg sodium, 2.6 g dietary fiber.

QUICK TIPS: Don't worry if the roast rests atop chunks of onion and carrot while it cooks. Press the pepper and mustard firmly into the meat.

Beef Kabobs with Vegetables

8 bamboo skewers

Nonstick spray

1 pound (455 g) rump roast, cut into 1-inch (2.5 cm) cubes

5 small potatoes, quartered

2 medium carrots, sliced ½ inch (13 mm) thick

2 medium onions, cut into wedges

1 can fat-free beef broth

1 tablespoon honey

¾ teaspoon ground cinnamon

⅛ teaspoon black pepper

⅛ teaspoon ground allspice and ⅛ teaspoon ground cloves

2 tablespoons garlic-flavored vinegar

1 can (6 ounces, 170 g) low-sodium tomato paste

Kabobs with a tasty twist: No-fuss slow-cooking replaces watch-'em-close grilling. Serve with a spinach salad with a tomato viniagrette.

MAKES 4 SERVINGS　　　　**LARGE RECTANGULAR CROCKERY POT**

Trim skewers to fit electric crockery pot. Coat a nonstick skillet with nonstick spray. Add meat and sauté it over medium-high heat until browned, about 6 minutes. Slide meat, potatoes, carrots, and onions onto skewers, alternating meat and vegetable pieces. Place in the bottom of a crockery pot.

In a bowl, combine the broth, honey, cinnamon, pepper, allspice, cloves, vinegar, and tomato paste. Mix well. Pour the broth mixture into the crockery pot and add enough water to barely cover the kabobs. Cover and cook on LOW until the vegetables are tender, 8 to 10 hours (on HIGH, 4 to 6 hours).

PER SERVING: About 338 calories, 5.6 g fat (15% of calories), 1.8 g saturated fat, 60 mg cholesterol, 156 mg sodium, 5.7 g dietary fiber.

COOK'S NOTE: No time for skewering meat and vegetables? That's okay. Simply skip that step and eliminate the added water. Voilà! A delicious, fast-to-fix stew.

Dijon Beef with Mushrooms

Olive-oil nonstick spray

¾ pound (340 g) beef round steak, cut into thin strips

8 ounces (228 g) mushrooms, sliced

6 cloves garlic, minced

1 cup (240 ml) fat-free beef broth

1 tablespoon red wine vinegar

1 tablespoon reduced-sodium soy sauce

¾ cup (180 g) nonfat sour cream

½ cup (53 g) chopped roasted red peppers

2 teaspoons Dijon mustard

¼ teaspoon white pepper

10 ounce (284 g) wide noodles

If you've been looking for a Stroganoff-style dish that's long on flavor but short on fat, this beef over noodles combo should fill the bill.

MAKES 4 SERVINGS　　　　**MEDIUM CROCKERY POT**

Coat a nonstick skillet with the spray and heat over medium-high heat. Add the beef, and sauté, stirring, until brown, 4 to 5 minutes. Remove to the crockery pot.

In the same skillet, sauté the mushrooms until lightly browned, about 3 minutes. Remove to the crockery pot and add the garlic, broth, vinegar, and soy sauce. Cover and cook on LOW until the beef is cooked through and very tender, 6 to 8 hours. Stir in the roasted peppers, sour cream, mustard, and white pepper. Cook, stirring, until heated through.

Meanwhile, cook the noodles according to package directions. Drain well and divide among 4 plates. Top with the beef mixture.

PER SERVING: 501 calories, 5.8 g fat (11% of calories), 1.6 g saturated fat, 71 mg cholesterol, 328 mg sodium, 2.6 g dietary fiber.

BEEF KABOBS WITH VEGETABLES

Pork Chops New Orleans

1 can (16 ounces, 455 g) stewed
tomatoes

Juice of 1 lemon

1 teaspoon Worcestershire sauce

Dash of Louisiana hot-pepper sauce

¼ cup (60 ml) dry white wine

Nonstick spray

1 medium onion, thinly sliced

1 sweet green pepper, thinly sliced

2 cloves garlic, minced

4 boneless center-cut loin pork chops,
trimmed of fat and cut
½-inch (13 mm) thick

Dash of white pepper

¼ cup (60 ml) *cold* water

2 tablespoons cornstarch

1 cup (200 g) rice

As in traditional Creole cooking, this palate-pleasing main course favors tomatoes, sweet peppers, and onions. Serve with slaw or steamed green beans or broccoli.

MAKES 4 SERVINGS   **MEDIUM CROCKERY POT**

Combine the tomatoes, lemon juice, Worcestershire sauce, hot-pepper sauce, and wine in a crockery pot.

Coat a nonstick skillet with the nonstick spray, and sauté the onions, green peppers, and garlic over medium-high heat until the onions are golden, 3 to 5 minutes. Transfer the onion mixture to the crockery pot and mix well.

In the same skillet, brown the pork on both sides over medium-high heat. Place the pork on top of the tomato-onion mixture. Sprinkle the pork with the white pepper. Cover and cook on LOW until the pork is tender, 8 to 10 hours. In the last half-hour, cook the rice separately; keep warm. Transfer the pork to a platter, leaving the tomato-onion mixture in the crockery pot. Keep the pork warm.

Combine the water and cornstarch in a measuring cup. Stir the cornstarch mixture into the tomato-onion mixture, and cook on LOW, stirring often, until the liquid thickens, 1 to 2 minutes. Divide the rice among four serving plates; top it with the tomato-onion mixture and a pork chop.

PER SERVING: About 436 calories, 13.4 g fat (28% of calories), 4.6 g saturated fat, 81 mg cholesterol, 98 mg sodium, 1.3 g dietary fiber.

COOK'S NOTE: What's the difference between Louisiana hot sauce and tabasco? Plenty of heat—that's what! Of the two, Louisiana is the milder. If you choose to use tabasco, measure it in drops, not teaspoonsful.

Beef and Corn Burritos

About 10 ounces (284 g) shredded beef brisket (page 134)

1 cup (142 g) frozen corn

1 large tomato, chopped

½ cup (120 ml) medium-hot salsa

1 teaspoon cumin seeds

½ cup (53 g) chopped roasted red peppers

4 large flour tortillas (10-inch, 25 cm) diameter)

¼ cup (27 g) shredded Monterey Jack cheese

½ cup (120 g) fat-free sour cream

MAKES 4 SERVINGS

Preheat oven to 350°F (176.6°C). Combine the beef, corn, tomatoes, salsa, cumin seeds, and red peppers in a saucepan. Cook over medium heat until hot, about 5 minutes.

Spread over the tortillas. Top with the cheese. Roll up. Place, seam side down, in a baking dish. Cover with foil. Heat in the oven until hot throughout, about 5 minutes. Top with sour cream.

PER SERVING: *329 calories, 8.1 g fat, 372 mg sodium, 4.4 g dietary fiber.*

JAMAICAN JERK PORK

Jamaican Jerk Pork

2 cups (480 ml) fat-free beef broth

2 teaspoons dried minced onions

1 teaspoon dried thyme

1 teaspoon garlic powder

1 teaspoon crushed red pepper flakes

¼ teaspoon ground cinnamon

¼ teaspoon powdered ginger

¼ teaspoon allspice

pinch of ground cloves

1 pound (455 g) pork tenderloin

3 tablespoons *cold* water

2 tablespoons cornstarch

This trendy entrée gets its flavorful, hot zing from a rub with eight spices, including pungent cloves and nippy peppers.

MAKES 4 SERVINGS   **MEDIUM CROCKERY POT**

Pour the broth into the crockery pot.

In a small bowl, combine the onions, thyme, garlic, red pepper flakes, cinnamon, ginger, allspice and cloves. Rub the spice mixture into all sides of the pork. Place the pork in the crockery pot.

Cover and cook on LOW until the pork is cooked through and a meat thermometer registers 160°F or 71.1°C, 6 to 8 hours. Let rest for 10 minutes before slicing and serving.

Remove to a platter, reserving the broth; keep the pork warm. Pour the broth into a saucepan.

In a small cup whisk together the cold water and cornstarch. Stir into the broth, and cook, stirring, over medium heat until slightly thickened. Slice the pork and serve topped with the thickened broth.

PER SERVING: 224 calories, 5.6 g fat (23% of calories), 1.9 g saturated fat, 89 mg cholesterol, 147 mg sodium, 0.4 g dietary fiber.

QUICK TIP: Some supermarkets carry jerk seasoning. If yours does, give the prepared combo a try.

Spicy Barbecue Beef

1 tablespoon tomato paste

1 cup (240 ml) no-salt-added
   tomato sauce

3 tablespoons dried minced onions

1 teaspoon olive oil

Juice of ½ lime

1 tablespoon light brown sugar

1 teaspoon horseradish mustard

About 10 ounces (284 g) shredded beef
   brisket (page 134)

¼ teaspoon liquid hickory smoke

4 Kaiser rolls, split

MAKES 4 SERVINGS   **MEDIUM CROCKERY POT**

Combine the tomato paste, tomato sauce, onions, oil, lime juice, brown sugar, mustard, and beef in the crockery pot. Cover and cook on LOW or HIGH until the flavors are blended, 3 to 4 hours on LOW or 2 to 3 hours on HIGH.

Stir in the liquid smoke. Spoon into the rolls.

PER SERVING: 336 calories, 8.1 g fat, 392 mg sodium, 2.7 g dietary fiber.

Beef Rolls with Pickles

4 very thin round beef steaks (total 1 pound, 455 g)

1 teaspoon Dijon-style mustard

1 carrot, halved lengthwise and crosswise

1 onion, quartered

2 small dill pickles, halved

Kitchen string

½ cup (120 ml) fat-free beef broth

1 teaspoon browning sauce

1 tablespoon red wine vinegar

⅛ teaspoon black pepper

¼ cup (60 ml) *cold* water

2 tablespoons cornstarch

Savor the piquant flavors of beef, vegetables, and pickles in this updated German classic. And be sure to sop up its delicious gravy with mashed potatoes or hearty whole grain bread.

MAKES 4 SERVINGS   **MEDIUM CROCKERY POT**

Pound the steaks to ⅛-inch (3 mm) thick; then spread ¼ teaspoon mustard on each. Place a carrot stick, onion quarter, and pickle half in the center of each steak. Roll up the steaks, and secure them with the string. Place the steak rolls in a crockery pot.

Combine the broth, browning sauce, vinegar, and black pepper in a measuring cup. Pour the broth mixture over the steak rolls in the crockery pot. Cover and cook on LOW for 6 to 8 hours or on HIGH for 4 to 6 hours. Transfer the beef rolls to a platter, leaving the liquid in the crockery pot. Keep the rolls warm. Combine the water and cornstarch in a measuring cup. Stir the cornstarch mixture into the gravy and cook, stirring often until the gravy thickens, 2 to 3 minutes. Serve the beef rolls topped with the gravy.

PER SERVING: About 209 calories, 6.8 g fat (30% of calories), 2.6 g saturated fat, 68 mg cholesterol, 533 mg sodium, 1.1 g dietary fiber.

COOK'S NOTE: Have metal skewers but no string? Use the skewers for securing the rolls. Carefully transfer the rolls to and from the crockery pot.

Hoisin Pork with Bamboo Shoots

1 pound (455 g) pork chops, cut into ¾-inch (20 mm) cubes

1 can (5 ounces, 142 g) sliced bamboo shoots, rinsed and drained

2 ribs celery, thinly sliced

1 small onion, cut into thin wedges

½ cup chopped roasted red pepper

1 cup (240 ml) fat-free beef broth

1 tablespoon hoisin sauce

8 ounces (228 g) rice sticks

Sweet–spicy and reddish brown in color, hoisin sauce brings authentic Chinese flavor to everyday pork. Bamboo shoots give the dish crunch while roasted red peppers provide a splash of color.

MAKES 6 SERVINGS   **MEDIUM CROCKERY POT**

Combine the pork, bamboo shoots, celery, onions, red peppers, broth, and hoisin sauce in the crockery pot. Cover and cook on LOW until the pork is tender, 5 to 6 hours on LOW or 3 to 4 hours on HIGH.

Meanwhile, cook the rice sticks according to package directions, and drain well. Add to the pork mixture, tossing to mix well. Serve immediately.

PER SERVING: 342 calories, 6.5 g fat, 126 mg sodium, 2.9 g dietary fiber.

QUICK TIPS: Select center-cut pork chops; they usually have the least waste and are, therefore, most reasonably priced. Use roasted red peppers from a jar to save time.

Pecan-Rubbed Pork

2¼ cups (540 ml) fat-free beef broth

Juice of 1 lemon

2 tablespoons chili sauce

3-pound (1.36 kg) pork sirloin roast, trimmed of fat

2 tablespoons pecans, ground

1 tablespoon yellow mustard seeds

1 tablespoon brown sugar

1 teaspoon grated lemon peel

¼ teaspoon freshly ground black pepper

4 russet potatoes, halved

Nuts about nuts? Then sample this pecan-encased pork roast. The meat is succulent; the pecan–mustard top has matchless flavor; and the potatoes are infused with a captivating chili broth.

MAKES 4 SERVINGS　　　　　　**MEDIUM CROCKERY POT**

Combine the broth, lemon juice, and chili sauce in the crockery pot. Place the pork in the crockery pot.

Combine the pecans, mustard seeds, brown sugar, lemon peel, and pepper in a small bowl; press into the pork above the liquid.

Cover and cook on LOW until the pork is cooked through and a meat thermometer registers 160°F or 71.1°C, 8 to 10 hours. Let rest for 10 minutes before slicing and serving.

Divide the roast into thirds. Freeze two-thirds for later use. Slice the remaining roast and serve with the potatoes.

PER SERVING: 341 calories, 9.7 g fat, 173 mg sodium, 2.5 g dietary fiber.

QUICK TIP: Store pecans in a covered container in the freezer, where they'll stay fresh for about a year.

Rich Red Sauce

2 teaspoons olive oil

½ pound (228 g) ground sirloin

1 onion, chopped

6 cloves garlic, minced

1 carrot, shredded

¼ cup (60 ml) dry red wine

1 tablespoon no-salt-added tomato paste

½ teaspoon Italian seasoning

¼ teaspoon freshly ground black pepper

1 can (28 ounces, 800 g) crushed tomatoes

½ cup (40 g) chopped fresh parsley

½ cup (43 g) freshly grated Provolone cheese

For pasta lovers: Here's a robust, meaty tomato sauce that will cling beautifully to your favorite pasta, be it spaghetti, fettucine, ziti, or rotelle. A shredded carrot sweetens the sauce, while Provolone cheese boosts flavor and richness.

MAKES 6 SERVINGS　　　　　　**MEDIUM CROCKERY POT**

Heat the oil in a large skillet over medium-high heat. Add the beef, onion, garlic, and carrots, and sauté, stirring, until the beef is crumbly and lightly browned and the onion is translucent.

Combine the wine, tomato paste, Italian seasoning, pepper, crushed tomatoes, and beef in the crockery pot. Cover and cook on LOW or HIGH until the flavors are blended, 5 to 6 hours on LOW or 3 to 4 hours on HIGH.

Stir in the cheese and parsley.

PER SERVING: 180 calories, 5 g fat, 408 mg sodium, 3.5 g dietary fiber.

QUICK TIP: Grated Romano or Parmesan cheese can be substituted for the Provolone.

Pork Tenderloin Teriyaki

1 tablespoon grated gingerroot

1 teaspoon minced garlic

¼ teaspoon freshly ground
    black pepper

1 cup (240 ml) fat-free beef broth

1 tablespoon reduced-sodium
    teriyaki sauce

¾ pound (340 g) pork tenderloin

1½ pounds (680 g) sweet potatoes,
    peeled and quartered

2 onions, cut into wedges

Here's a dinner of pork and sweet potatoes that's so tasty it can't be ignored. I usually use the large red variety of sweet potatoes, but the smaller yellow-fleshed variety is also noteworthy. Serve with peas, green beans, or a tossed salad.

MAKES 4 SERVINGS   **MEDIUM CROCKERY POT**

Combine the gingerroot, garlic, pepper, and teriyaki in a small bowl. Rub over the pork. Pour the broth into the crockery pot and add the pork (if necessary, halve the pork so it fits in the crockery pot). Arrange the potatoes and onions around the edges.

Cover and cook on LOW until the pork is cooked through and a meat thermometer registers 160°F or 71.1°C, 6 to 8 hours. Let rest for 10 minutes before slicing and serving.

PER SERVING: 354 calories, 8.2 g fat, 330 mg sodium, 4.5 g dietary fiber.

QUICK TIP: Sweet potatoes don't store as well as their white cousins. Keep in a cool dry place, don't refrigerate, and use within a week.

Meat Loaf with Carrots and Onions

1 cup (200 g) finely chopped tomatoes

4 sprigs of fresh parsley, finely chopped,
    or 4 tablespoons dried

3 egg whites, beaten

¼ teaspoon freshly ground
    black pepper

1 medium onion, shredded

1 dried cayenne pepper, minced, or
    ½ teaspoon crushed red
    pepper flakes

2 cups (280 g) dry bread crumbs

½ cup (120 ml) ketchup

6 fresh sage leaves, snipped, or
    1 teaspoon dried sage

2 medium carrots, finely shredded

½ cup (70 g) corn

1 tablespoon red wine vinegar

1 pound (455 g) extra-lean
    ground round

1 cup (240 ml) fat-free beef broth

1 cup (240 ml) water

Remember Mom's delicious, home-style meat loaf? It's here. Prepare it early in the day so it is ready to eat when you are.

MAKES 8 SERVINGS   **LARGE CROCKERY POT WITH STEAMING RACK**

Combine the tomatoes, parsley, egg whites, black pepper, onions, cayenne pepper, bread crumbs, ¼ cup (60 ml) ketchup, sage, carrots, corn, and vinegar in a large bowl. Add the ground beef and mix thoroughly.

Place a steaming rack or metal vegetable steaming basket in crockery pot. Pour the broth and water into the crockery pot. Shape the beef mixture into an oblong or round loaf, depending on the crockery pot's shape, and place the loaf on the rack. Cover and cook on HIGH until the meat is done, 4 to 6 hours. Brush the remaining ketchup over the meat loaf. Cover and cook 15 minutes.

PER SERVING: About 310 calories, 12 g fat (34% of calories), 4.2 g saturated fat, 38 mg cholesterol, 386 mg sodium, 3.1 g dietary fiber.

PORK TENDERLOIN TERIYAKI

Beer-Braised Pot Roast

Cooking spray

2 pounds (910 g) top round beef roast, trimmed of visible fat

6 onions, quartered

6 cloves garlic, pressed

8 ounces (228 g) mushrooms, quartered

12 ounces (360 ml) nonalcoholic beer

1 bay leaf

½ cup (120 ml) *cold* water

¼ teaspoon ground turmeric

Pinch of ground cinnamon

2 teaspoons browning and seasoning sauce

¼ cup (35 g) flour

16 ounces (455 g) wide noodles

Not your run-of-the-mill pot roast: this one sports a piquant, full-bodied gravy that's seasoned with garlic, bay leaf, cinnamon, and turmeric.

MAKES 8 SERVINGS　　　　　　　**MEDIUM CROCKERY POT**

Coat a nonstick skillet with the cooking spray, and heat over medium-high heat. Add the beef, and cook, stirring occasionally, until brown, 5 to 10 minutes. Remove to the crockery pot and add the onions, garlic, mushrooms, beer, and bay leaf. Cover and cook on LOW until the beef is very tender and a meat thermometer registers at least 160°F or 71.1°C, 8 to 10 hours.

Remove the beef to a platter, reserving the beer-onion mixture; keep the beef warm. Discard the bay leaf. Pour the beer-onion mixture into a saucepan.

In a small measuring cup, combine the water, turmeric, cinnamon, browning sauce, and flour. Pour into the beer–onion mixture and cook, stirring, over medium heat until thickened.

Meanwhile, cook the noodles according to package directions. Drain well.

Slice the beef, and serve with the beer–onion mixture and noodles.

PER SERVING: 443 calories, 7.1 g fat (15% of calories), 2.2 g saturated fat, 53 mg cholesterol, 111 mg sodium, 3.8 g dietary fiber.

QUICK TIP: Use regular beer or ale, if you wish.

Roast Leg of Lamb Provençal

3 pounds (1.36 kg) lamb shank

1 teaspoon olive oil

1 teaspoon herbes de Provence

4 cloves garlic, sliced

1 cup (240 ml) fat-free beef broth

1 tablespoon dry red wine

A sophisticated entrée, this tender leg of lamb begs for inclusion in company-special dinners. Present it with mashed garlic potatoes or a rice pilaf and a green vegetable such as broccoli, asparagus, or peas.

MAKES 8 SERVINGS　　　　　　　**LARGE CROCKERY POT**

Coat a large nonstick skillet with cooking spray and heat over high heat. Add the lamb and cook, turning often, until brown on all sides, 5 to 10 minutes. Let cool slightly.

Combine the oil and herbes de Provence in a small bowl. Cut small slits in the lamb. Stuff with the garlic slices. Rub the herbes de Provence mixture over the lamb.

Pour the broth and wine into the crockery pot. Add the lamb. Cover and cook on LOW until the lamb is cooked through and a meat thermometer registers at least 160°F or 71.1°C, 8 to 10 hours. Let rest for 10 minutes before slicing and serving.

PER SERVING: 319 calories, 11.9 g fat, 133 mg sodium, 0.1 g dietary fiber.

QUICK TIP: Use a sharp paring knife to cut the slits in the lamb.

German-Style Sauerbraten

1 cup (240 ml) fat-free beef broth

1 large onion, cut into thin wedges

2 cloves garlic, minced

1 teaspoon mixed peppercorns (sometimes called pepper melange)

1 tablespoon pickling spice

1 bay leaf

2 cups (480 ml) dry red wine

1 teaspoon coriander seeds

1 pound (455 g) beef rump roast, trimmed of fat

½ cup (about 12 cookies) gingersnap crumbs

½ cup (120 g) fat-free sour cream

Traditional sauerbraten simmers for hours on the stove top. This oven version has been simplified, and features the same great flavors found in classic recipes.

MAKES 4 SERVINGS　　　　　　　**MEDIUM CROCKERY POT**

In a glass bowl, combine the broth, onions, garlic, peppercorns, pickling spice, bay leaf, wine, and coriander. Add the beef. Cover and marinate in the refrigerator for 24 hours, turning once or twice.

Remove the beef and marinade to the crockery pot. Cover and cook on LOW until the beef is very tender and a meat thermometer registers at least 160°F or 71.1°C, 8 to 10 hours.

Remove the beef to a platter, reserving the broth mixture, and cover to keep warm. Pour the broth mixture through a strainer into a 2-quart (liter) saucepan. Discard the spices and onions. Stir the gingersnaps into the broth. Cook, stirring, over medium heat until thickened. Stir in the sour cream.

Slice the meat and serve topped with the broth mixture.

PER SERVING: 388 calories, 7.2 g fat, 295 mg sodium, 1.9 g dietary fiber.

QUICK TIP: Whole peppercorns, whole allspice, and whole mustard seeds can be substituted for the mixed peppercorns and pickling spice.

CORNED BEEF WITH RED CABBAGE

Corned Beef with Red Cabbage

1½ pound (680 g) corned eye of round beef, trimmed of fat

6½ cups (1.5 l) water

4 bay leaves

9 peppercorns

¼ cup (60 ml) red wine vinegar

6 russet potatoes

6 cups coarsely sliced red cabbage

Corned beef and cabbage, cooked in a crockery pot? Absolutely. The meat is deliciously tender and the flavors are superb. Oh, and you don't need to wait until St. Patrick's day to serve this delightful dinner.

MAKES 6 SERVINGS　　　　　　　　　　**MEDIUM CROCKERY POT**

Combine the beef, water, bay leaves, peppercorns, and vinegar in the crockery pot. Arrange the potatoes around the beef. Cover and cook on LOW until the beef is very tender and a meat thermometer registers at least 160°F or 71.1°C, 8 to 10 hours.

Add the cabbage, cover, and cook until tender, about 15 minutes. Discard the bay leaves.

PER SERVING: 325 calories, 4.5 g fat, 729 mg sodium, 5.5 g dietary fiber.

QUICK TIP: So the cabbage pieces stay together during cooking, leave a bit of core with each slice or wedge.

Pork Chops in Dill Sauce

1 can (14 ounces, 420 ml) fat-free beef broth

cooking spray

4 center cut loin pork chops (about 1 pound, 910 g), trimmed of visible fat

1 onion, chopped

1 bay leaf

4 potatoes, peeled and halved

¼ teaspoon freshly ground black pepper

1 tablespoon snipped fresh dill or 1 teaspoon dried

2 tablespoons cornstarch

Dill's a delicate herb that marries well with lean pork; stir it into this and other recipes toward the end of cooking to get its full lemony essence.

MAKES 4 SERVINGS　　　　　　　　　　**MEDIUM CROCKERY POT**

Pour 1½ cups (360 ml) of the broth into the crockery pot. Coat a nonstick skillet with the cooking spray and Heat over medium-high heat. Add the pork, and cook until brown on both sides, 4 to 6 minutes. Remove to the crockery pot. Add the onion, bay leaf, and potatoes.

Cover and cook on LOW or HIGH until the pork is cooked through, the potatoes are tender, and the flavors are blended, 5 to 6 hours on LOW or 3 to 4 hours on HIGH.

Remove the pork and potatoes to a platter, reserving the broth and onion; keep hot. Pour the broth and onion into a saucepan.

Whisk together the pepper, dill, cornstarch, and remaining broth. Pour into the broth–onion mixture, and cook, stirring, over medium heat until slightly thickened, 1 to 3 minutes. Serve over the pork and potatoes.

PER SERVING: 371 calories, 6.4 g fat (16% of calories), 2.3 g saturated fat, 61 mg cholesterol, 124 mg sodium, 6.2 g dietary fiber.

QUICK TIP: Avoid cooking the cornstarch-thickened sauce too long or stirring it too vigorously, or it will thin.

Heritage Pork Roast

½ cup (120 ml) apple juice or cider

1½ pounds (680 g) sweet potatoes, peeled and sliced 1 inch (2.5 cm) thick

3 medium onions, sliced and separated into rings

4 medium apples, peeled and sliced

2 pound (910 g) center-cut boneless pork roast, trimmed of fat

1 teaspoon Dijon mustard

¼ teaspoon black pepper

4 fresh sage leaves, snipped, or ⅛ teaspoon dried sage

¼ cup (60 ml) *cold* water

1 teaspoon brown sugar

2 tablespoons cornstarch

A braised roast with mustard-sage seasoning and a side of apple-flavored sweet potatoes. Serve with a light spinach salad.

MAKES 6 SERVINGS   **LARGE CROCKERY POT**

Pour the apple juice into a crockery pot. Then layer the sweet potatoes, onions, and apples in the crockery pot.

In a nonstick skillet, brown the pork on all sides over medium-high heat. Place the pork on top of the potato and apple slices. Brush the mustard over the roast and sprinkle the roast with the pepper and sage. Cover and cook on LOW until the roast is done and registers 165°F (73.9°C) on a quick reading meat thermometer, 7 to 9 hours.

Transfer the roast to a platter and keep it warm. Using a slotted spoon, transfer the apple–sweet potato mixture to a bowl and keep it warm.

Combine the water, sugar, and cornstarch in a measuring cup. Stir the cornstarch mixture into the juices in the crockery pot, and cook, stirring often, until they thicken, 1 to 2 minutes. Serve it over the apple-potato mixture and the roast.

PER SERVING: About 426 calories, 11.8 g fat (25% of calories), 3.5 g saturated fat, 88 mg cholesterol, 179 mg sodium, 4.4 g dietary fiber.

COOK'S NOTE: Don't be surprised if the apples seem to disappear during cooking; their wonderful, sweet flavor remains.

Shredded Beef

2½ pounds (1.14 kg) flat beef brisket, trimmed of fat

2½ cups (540 ml) water

1 onion, cut into thin wedges

4 cloves garlic, sliced

1 bay leaf

1 tablespoon pickling spice

½ cup (120 ml) cider vinegar

1 teaspoon coriander seeds

Three for one. That's what you'll get when you prepare this tender shredded beef. Cook up the beef, then use it to prepare Beef and Corn Burritos, Spicy Barbecue Beef, and Beef Stir-Fry with Black Bean Sauce.

MEDIUM CROCKERY POT

Combine the beef, water, onion, garlic, bay leaf, pickling spice, vinegar, and coriander seeds in the crockery pot. Cover and cook on LOW until the beef is are very tender and a meat thermometer registers at least 160°F or 71.1°C, 8 to 10 hours.

Remove to a platter and let cool slightly. Shred the beef, discarding fat. Divide into thirds. Use one-third to make each of the recipes listed in the note above. Discard the cooking liquid and spices.

HERITAGE PORK ROAST

Southwest Roast Dinner

1 can (14 ounces, 420 ml) fat-free
  beef broth

1 tablespoon red wine vinegar

1 cup (240 ml) water

2 pounds (910 g) bottom round roast,
  trimmed of fat

¼ teaspoon freshly ground
  black pepper

1 teaspoon cumin seeds

4 carrots, sliced ½ inch (13 cm) thick

2 potatoes, peeled and quartered

1 large onion, thickly sliced and
  separated into rings

4 ounces (114 g) mushroom caps

1 teaspoon liquid mesquite smoke

Better beef. Cumin and mesquite smoke, instead of the usual celery and black pepper, flavor this pot roast and potatoes dish. The meat cooks unattended for several hours until it's fork-tender. It's well worth the wait.

MAKES 6 SERVINGS   **MEDIUM CROCKERY POT**

Combine the broth, vinegar, and water in the crockery pot. Add the beef and season with pepper and cumin seeds. Arrange the carrots, potatoes, onions, and mushrooms, in the order listed, around the beef. Cover and cook on LOW until the beef is very tender and a meat thermometer registers at least 160°F or 71.1°C, 8 to 10 hours.

Remove the beef and vegetables to a serving platter, reserving the liquid. Spoon the liquid smoke over the meat. Cover with foil to keep warm and let rest for 10 minutes.

Skim the fat from the reserved cooking liquid. Slice the roast. Serve topped with the reserved liquid and accompanied with the vegetables.

PER SERVING: 376 calories, 7 g fat, 173 mg sodium, 5.2 g dietary fiber.

Veal Piccata

¾ cup (180 ml) fat-free chicken broth

¼ cup (60 ml) dry white wine

4 shallots, sliced

Olive-oil cooking spray

1 pound (455 g) veal cutlets

Juice of ½ lemon

¼ teaspoon freshly ground
  black pepper

1 tablespoon snipped fresh parsley

In this version of piccata, a classic dish hailing from Italy, dry white wine and shallots complement the traditional ingredients of veal, lemon, and parsley.

MAKES 4 SERVINGS   **MEDIUM CROCKERY POT**

Place the broth, wine, and shallots in the crockery pot.

Coat a nonstick skillet with the cooking spray and heat over medium-high heat. Add the veal and cook until browned on both sides, about 5 minutes. Remove to the crockery pot.

Cover and cook on LOW until the veal is cooked through and the flavors are blended, 4 to 6 hours.

Remove the veal to a platter, reserving the broth and shallots; keep the veal warm. Pour the lemon juice and pepper into the broth. Cook until heated through, about 5 minutes. Serve the veal topped with the shallots, broth, and parsley.

PER SERVING: 166 calories, 4 g fat (22% of calories), 1.6 g saturated fat, 87 mg cholesterol, 92 mg sodium, 0.6 g dietary fiber.

QUICK TIP: Use freshly ground black pepper whenever you can; it has more zip and zing than the preground variety.

Paprika Veal with White Beans

½ cup (120 ml) dry white wine

1 pound (455 g) veal sirloin

2 tablespoons balsamic vinegar

4 cloves garlic, pressed

2 teaspoons paprika

2 leeks, white part only, sliced

1 sweet red pepper, sliced

2 slices crisp-cooked bacon, crumbled

1 can (14 ounces, 400 g) great northern
beans, rinsed and drained

Fresh basil leaves, for garnish

A boldly seasoned paste of garlic and paprika flavors this tender veal sirloin. Enjoy it with the accompanying mild-flavored, fiber-rich beans and strips of sweet red pepper.

MAKES 4 SERVINGS   **LARGE CROCKERY POT**

Pour the wine into a crockery pot. Add the veal.

In a measuring cup, combine the vinegar, garlic, and paprika. Using a pastry brush, paint the veal with the vinegar-garlic mixture. Top the veal with the leeks, peppers, and bacon. Place the beans in the wine around the veal. Cover and cook on LOW until the veal is cooked through, 8 to 10 hours.

PER SERVING: About 436 calories, 9 g fat (19% of calories), 3.4 g saturated fat, 121 mg cholesterol, 169 mg sodium, 6.3 g dietary fiber.

COOK'S NOTE: Rinsing canned beans helps reduce the sodium level.

Veal Chops with Olives and Capers

Cooking spray

2 pounds (910 g) veal shoulder chops

1 cup (240 ml) fat-free beef broth

4 cloves garlic, minced

1 small onion, chopped

1 tablespoon finely chopped
Canadian bacon

1 tablespoon minced black olives

2 teaspoons capers, rinsed

3 tablespoons *cold* water

2 tablespoons cornstarch

Here's an enticing entrée that's sophisticated enough for a company dinner yet simple enough for an everyday supper, thanks to a special blend of bacon, capers, and olives.

MAKES 4 SERVINGS   **MEDIUM CROCKERY POT**

Coat a nonstick skillet with the cooking spray and heat over medium-high heat. Add the veal, and cook until brown on both sides. Remove to the crockery pot. Add the broth, garlic, onion, and bacon.

Cover and cook on LOW or HIGH until the veal is cooked through, the potatoes are tender, and the flavors are blended, 5 to 6 hours on LOW or 3 to 4 hours on HIGH.

Remove the veal to a platter, reserving the broth mixture. Keep the veal warm. Pour the broth mixture into a saucepan.

In a cup, whisk together the cold water and the cornstarch. Stir the olives, capers, and cornstarch mixture into the broth mixture. Cook, stirring, over medium heat until slightly thickened, 1 to 3 minutes. Serve over the veal.

PER SERVING: 268 calories, 8.7 g fat (30% of calories), 3.2 g saturated fat, 150 mg cholesterol, 292 mg sodium, 0.5 g dietary fiber.

QUICK TIPS: You can substitute green olives for the black ones in this recipe; just be aware that the green variety has more sodium. And remember to rinse capers to remove excess sodium before using them.

Basil Meatballs in Tomato Sauce

¾ pound (340 g) ground sirloin

½ cup (40 ml) quick oats

1 teaspoon dried oregano

¼ cup (15 ml) chopped fresh
    basil leaves

1 egg white

¼ cup (20 g) grated Romano cheese

¼ cup (35 g) unbleached flour

2 tablespoons olive oil

1 can (28 ounces, 800 g) crushed
    tomatoes

1 onion, chopped

4 cloves garlic, minced

¼ cup (60 ml) dry red wine

Generous amounts of basil brighten the flavor of these traditional beef favorites. Serve over spaghetti or in rolls. The hearty meatballs be an instant hit.

MAKES 4 SERVINGS　　　　　　　　　**MEDIUM CROCKERY POT**

Combine the beef, oats, Italian seasoning, basil, egg white, and cheese in a large bowl. Form into 1-inch (2.5 cm) balls and dredge in the flour.

Heat the oil in a large nonstick skillet over medium-high heat. Add the meatballs and cook, turning frequently, until browned, about 10 minutes.

Combine the tomatoes, onion, garlic, wine and meatballs in the crockery pot. Cover and cook on LOW or HIGH until the meatballs are cooked through and the flavors are blended, 5 to 6 hours on LOW or 3 to 4 hours on HIGH.

PER SERVING: 332 calories, 9 g fat, 654 mg sodium, 5.3 g dietary fiber.

QUICK TIPS: Form very firm meatballs and let them cook for several minutes before turning. That way, they won't fall apart.

These meatballs freeze quite nicely for up to a month. So why not double the recipe and freeze half for another day?

Mesquite Barbecue Beef on Rolls

1 pound (455 g) extra-lean ground beef

2 medium onions, finely chopped

1 medium sweet green pepper, chopped

1 clove garlic, minced

1½ cup (360 ml) Slow-Cooked Barbecue
    Sauce (see page 75) or store-
    bought barbecue sauce

1 can (15 ounces, 426 g) pinto beans,
    rinsed and drained

½ teaspoon mesquite or other
    liquid smoke

8 whole wheat Kaiser rolls

Holy smokes! Here's a speedy hot sandwich with enough robust taste to satisfy the heartiest appetites.

MAKES 4 SERVINGS　　　　　　　　　**MEDIUM CROCKERY POT**

Cook the beef in a nonstick skillet over medium-high heat until brown and crumbly, 4 to 6 minutes. Using a slotted spoon, transfer the beef to a crockery pot. Pour off and discard the drippings.

In the same skillet, sauté the onions and green peppers until translucent, 3 to 5 minutes. Transfer to the crockery pot. Stir in the garlic, barbecue sauce, beans, and liquid smoke. Cover and cook on LOW for 7 to 10 hours. Serve in the rolls.

PER SERVING: About 366 calories, 12 g fat (30% calories), 4.2 g saturated fat, 38 mg cholesterol, 462 mg sodium, 3 g dietary fiber.

COOK'S NOTE: For even less fat, make this meaty dish with ground turkey breast.

BASIL MEATBALLS IN RED SAUCE

Lemon-Onion Pork Chops

1 cup (200 g) canned crushed tomatoes with basil

4 boneless ½-inch-thick (13 mm) center-cut loin pork chops, trimmed of fat

Freshly ground black pepper

1 lemon, cut into 4 slices

1 medium onion, cut into 4 slices

4 sprigs of fresh thyme or lemon thyme, or ½ teaspoon dried thyme

1 bay leaf

4 scrubbed potatoes, in their jackets

The tangy flavor of lemon prevails in this delicious, fast-to-prepare dish. Serve with spinach salad topped with a fat-free blue cheese dressing or steamed French-cut green beans.

MAKES 4 SERVINGS　　　　**MEDIUM CROCKERY POT**

Spoon half the tomatoes into a crockery pot. Arrange the pork chops in a single layer over the tomatoes. Sprinkle with the pepper. Top each chop with a lemon slice and an onion slice. Add the thyme and bay leaf. Spoon the remaining tomatoes over the chops. Cover and cook on LOW until the pork is tender, 7 to 9 hours.

In the oven, bake the potatoes at 425°F (218°C) until done, about 1 hour, or microwave on HIGH, turning once, for 20 minutes. Discard the thyme and bay leaf. Serve the lemony tomato sauce over the chops and potatoes.

PER SERVING: About 325 calories, 7 g fat (20% of calories), 2.5 g saturated fat, 61 mg cholesterol, 224 mg sodium, 3.5 g dietary fiber.

COOK'S NOTES: The chops and sauce can be frozen for up to a month. To reheat them, thaw them in the refrigerator, then heat them until the pork is hot and the sauce is hot and bubbly throughout.

Potatoes develop a mealy texture when frozen, so cook fresh potatoes right before serving.

Beef with Red Wine Gravy

Olive-oil cooking spray

2½ pound (1.14 kg) eye of round beef roast, trimmed of fat

2 onions, cut into thin wedges

4 ounces (114 g) mushrooms, sliced

1 can (14 ounces (420 ml)) fat-free beef broth

¼ cup (60 ml) dry red wine

4 cloves garlic, minced

¼ cup (60 ml) *cold* water

2½ tablespoons instant flour

1 teaspoon browning and seasoning sauce

Extra-lean eye of round adapts beautifully to slow cooking, and a two-pound (910g) roast, including a gravy that boasts red wine, mushrooms and onions is ready to eat when you are.

MAKES 8 SERVINGS　　　　**MEDIUM CROCKERY POT**

Coat a nonstick skillet with the cooking spray, and heat over medium-high heat. Add the beef, and cook, turning often, until well browned on all sides, 5 to 10 minutes. Remove to the crockery pot.

In the same skillet, sauté the onions and mushrooms, stirring, until lightly browned, about 4 minutes. Remove to the crockery pot. Add the broth, wine, and garlic. Cover and cook on LOW until the beef is very tender and a meat thermometer registers at least 160°F or 71.1°C, 8 to 10 hours.

Remove the beef to a platter, reserving the broth and vegetables; keep the beef warm. Pour the broth and vegetables into a saucepan.

In a small measuring cup, combine the flour, water, and seasoning sauce. Stir into the broth–vegetable mixture. Cook, stirring, over medium heat until thickened. Slice the beef and serve topped with the broth-vegetable mixture.

PER SERVING: 229 calories, 5.5 g fat (22% of calories), 2 g saturated fat, 78 mg cholesterol, 109 mg sodium, 0.9 g dietary fiber.

Quick Beef-and-Lentil Tacos

1 pound (455 g) extra-lean ground beef

2 medium onions, chopped

½ sweet green pepper, chopped

1 carrot, finely shredded

4 cloves garlic, minced

1⅓ cups (267 g) crushed tomatoes

1⅓ cups (267 g) dry lentils

1 cup (240 ml) water

1 tablespoon chili powder

1 teaspoon ground cumin

16 soft flour taco shells or flour tortillas

1 or 2 jalapeño peppers, minced (optional)

FOR GARNISH:

1 cup (110 g) shredded Monterey Jack cheese

Torn lettuce

1 large tomato, chopped

Medium-hot or hot salsa

The heat's up, but not too much. These Tex-Mex tacos are boldly seasoned with chili, yet remain palate cool 'n' friendly. Serve with crisp vegetable crudités, such as carrots, sweet peppers, cauliflower, and broccoli.

MAKES 4 SERVINGS   **MEDIUM CROCKERY POT**

Brown the beef in a large nonstick skillet over medium-high heat, 5 to 7 minutes. Using a slotted spoon, transfer the beef to a crockery pot. With paper towels, wipe most of the fat from the skillet, then add the onions and green pepper. Cook until the onions are translucent, about 5 minutes.

Transfer the onion mixture to the crockery pot. Stir in the carrots, garlic, tomatoes, lentils, water, chili powder, and cumin. Cover and cook on LOW until the lentils are tender, 6 to 8 hours.

Spoon the beef-lentil mixture into the taco shells, and fold the shells in half. Place the filled shells on a baking sheet, and cover them with foil. Warm in a 325°F (163°C) oven for 5 minutes. Garnish each taco with the cheese, lettuce, tomatoes, and salsa.

PER TACO: About 254 calories, 7.6 g fat, (27% of calories), 2.3 g saturated fat, 19 mg cholesterol, 241 mg sodium, 0.8 g. dietary fiber.

COOK'S NOTES: For fiery hot tacos, add one or two minced jalapeño peppers during the last hour of cooking.

You can refrigerate the beef-lentil mixture for up to 3 days. When you are ready to serve it, heat it until hot throughout, then spoon it into the shells. Warm the shells; then garnish as in the recipe.

BEEF ROAST WITH MUSHROOM-ONION GRAVY

Beef Roast with Mushroom-Onion Gravy

3 pounds (1.36 kg) bottom-round beef, trimmed of fat

3 medium onions, finely chopped

8 ounces (228 g) mushrooms, thickly sliced

Butter-flavored nonstick spray

½ cup (120 ml) dry red wine

¼ teaspoon black pepper

¼ cup (60 ml) *cold* water

2 tablespoons cornstarch

1 teaspoon browning sauce

Pot roast never tasted so good or was so easy to prepare. Serve with HARVEST POTATOES (see page 84) and a green vegetable.

MAKES 12 SERVINGS　　　　　　　**LARGE CROCKERY POT**

Brown the roast on all sides in a nonstick skillet over medium-high heat, 5 to 6 minutes; transfer to a crockery pot. In the skillet, sauté the onions until golden, about 3 minutes; transfer them to the crockery pot. Add the mushrooms to the same skillet, lightly coat with spray; sauté until golden, about 3 minutes. Transfer the mushrooms to the crockery pot.

Pour the wine into the crockery pot; sprinkle the roast with the pepper. Cover and cook on LOW until the roast is tender, 8 to 10 hours. Transfer the roast to a platter, leaving the onions, the mushrooms and liquid in the crockery pot. Keep the roast warm.

Combine the cold water, cornstarch and browning sauce in a measuring cup. Stir the cornstarch mixture into the onion-mushroom gravy, and cook, stirring often, until the gravy thickens, 2 to 3 minutes. Slice the roast; serve topped with gravy.

PER SERVING: About 245 calories, 8.5 g fat (32% of calories), 2.9 g saturated fat, 88 mg cholesterol, 95 mg sodium, 0.9 g dietary fiber.

COOK'S NOTE: The meat freezes well for up to a month. The gravy, once thickened with cornstarch, won't freeze well, but it'll keep in the refrigerator for a day or two.

Lime–Salsa Pork Chops

1 cup (240 ml) low-sodium vegetable juice

4 boneless center-cut loin pork chops (about 1 pound, 455 g), trimmed of fat

½ teaspoon lemon pepper

1 lime, cut into 8 slices

1 onion, cut into 8 slices

1 cup (240 ml) medium-hot salsa

4 sprigs fresh thyme or ½ teaspoon dried

4 red potatoes, halved

In this dynamite dish, the familiar flavors of lime, onions, and tomatoes complement succulent pork while hot, tender potatoes soak up all the intriguing flavors. Serve with a tossed salad or hot green vegetable.

MAKES 4 SERVINGS　　　　　　　**MEDIUM CROCKERY POT**

Pour the juice into the crockery pot and arrange the pork chops in the bottom. Sprinkle lemon pepper over them. Arrange 2 slices of lime and onion atop each. Top with the salsa and thyme. Arrange the potatoes around the chops. Cover and cook on LOW until the chops are cooked through and the potatoes are tender, 5 to 6 hours.

Discard the thyme sprigs. Serve the chops topped with the lime, onions, and salsa. Top the potatoes with the salsa.

PER SERVING: 316 calories, 7.5 g fat, 360 mg sodium, 3.6 g dietary fiber.

Gingered Pork Over Rice

3 cups (720 ml) fat-free beef broth

Butter-flavored cooking spray

1 pound (455 g) center-cut pork chops, cut into ¾-inch (20 mm) cubes

3 tablespoons apple juice

1 tablespoon reduced-sodium soy sauce

6 cloves garlic, minced

1 tablespoon minced gingerroot

2 tablespoons cornstarch

4 tablespoons *cold* water

1 cup (200 g) wild pecan rice or white long-grain rice

Snipped fresh parsley, garnish

Here's a dish that sports the signature tastes of an Asian stir-fry: salty (soy sauce), spicy (gingerroot), and sweet (apple juice).

MAKES 4 SERVINGS   **MEDIUM CROCKERY POT**

Coat a nonstick skillet with the cooking spray and heat over medium-high heat. Add the pork, and cook until brown, 3 to 5 minutes. Remove to the crockery pot. Add 1 cup (240 ml) of the broth, the juice, soy sauce, garlic and gingerroot. Cover and cook on LOW until the pork is cooked through and tender, 5 to 6 hours.

Combine the water and cornstarch in a small measuring cup. Pour into the pork mixture. Cook, stirring, until slightly thickened, 5 to 10 minutes.

Meanwhile, in a 3-quart (liter) pot, bring the remaining 2 cups (480 ml) broth to a boil. Stir in the rice, reduce the heat, and cook until the rice is tender and the liquid has been absorbed, about 20 minutes. Divide among 4 plates and top with the pork and thickened broth. Garnish with the parsley.

PER SERVING: 417 calories, 9.6 g fat (21% of calories), 3.4 g saturated fat, 93 mg cholesterol, 343 mg sodium, 2.7 g dietary fiber.

QUICK TIP: Stash gingerroot in a cool, dry place or freeze it. To freeze the root, pare off the papery skin and place the root in a plastic bag.

Swedish Meatballs

1 cup (240 ml) fat-free beef broth

¼ pound (114 g) ground round beef

¼ pound (114 g) ground pork

½ cup (40 g) quick-cooking oats

1 egg white

2 tablespoons dried minced onions

1 tablespoon dried parsley

¾ teaspoon allspice

½ teaspoon ground nutmeg

½ teaspoon Worcestershire sauce

8 ounces (228 g) wide noodles

½ cup (120 g) nonfat sour cream

That classic of the holiday buffet, Swedish meatballs, with their singular allspice and nutmeg seasoning, makes for a delightfully quick and delicious dinner.

MAKES 4 SERVINGS   **MEDIUM CROCKERY POT**

Pour the broth into the crockery pot.

Combine the beef, pork, oats, egg white, onions, parsley, allspice, nutmeg, and Worcestershire sauce in a large bowl. Form the mixture into 16 walnut-size balls. Coat a a nonstick skillet with cooking spray and heat over medium-high heat. Add the meatballs and cook, turning occasionally, until browned, 5 to 8 minutes. Remove to the crockery pot. Cover and cook on LOW or HIGH until the meatballs are cooked through and the flavors are blended, 5 to 6 hours on LOW or 3 to 4 hours on HIGH.

Remove the meatballs to a platter, reserving the broth. Stir the sour cream into the broth.

Cook the noodles according to package directions. Drain well and divide among 4 plates. Serve topped with the meatballs and sour cream mixture.

PER SERVING: 416 calories, 6.9 g fat (15% of calories), 2.2 g saturated fat, 49 mg cholesterol, 145 mg sodium, 2.8 g dietary fiber.

QUICK TIP: For maximum flavor, the meatballs should be well-browned.

Sweet and Sour Beef

Nonstick spray

½ pound (228 g) rump roast, cut into 1-inch (2.5 cm) cubes

1 orange, sections cut into 1-inch (2.5 cm) cubes

1 cup (228 g) dried apricot halves

2 small onions, cut into thin wedges

1 cup (171 g) chopped sweet green pepper

1 cup (240 ml) fat-free beef broth

2 tablespoons apple cider vinegar

2 tablespoons low-sodium soy sauce

1 tablespoon honey

⅛ teaspoon ground red pepper

2 teaspoons arrowroot starch

2 tablespoons *cold* water

8 ounces (228 g) medium egg noodles

Honey and vinegar, vegetables, and fruit provide the wonderfully complex flavors in this one-dish dinner. Bonus: Fiber's high; calories and fat are low.

MAKES 4 SERVINGS   **MEDIUM CROCKERY POT**

Coat a nonstick skillet with nonstick spray. Add the meat and sauté it over medium-high heat until browned, about 5 minutes. Transfer it to a crockery pot. Add the apricots, onions, and green peppers.

Stir in the broth, vinegar, soy sauce, honey, and red pepper. Cover and cook on LOW for 6 to 7 hours or on HIGH for 3½ to 5 hours. During the last half-hour, make the egg noodles separately and drain; keep them warm.

Dissolve the arrowroot in the cold water. Stir the arrowroot mixture into the broth mixture in the crockery pot, and cook until the sauce is slightly thickened, about 4 minutes. Serve over the hot noodles.

PER SERVING: About 441 calories, 3.7 g fat (7% of calories), 1.0 g saturated fat, 30 mg cholesterol, 364 mg sodium, 5.1 g dietary fiber.

COOK'S NOTE: Can't find any arrowroot? Thicken the sauce with cornstarch instead.

Mushroom-Stuffed Beef Roll-Ups

4 thin beef round steaks (about
    3 ounces, 85 g each)

Olive-oil cooking spray

4 ounces (114 g) mushrooms, chopped

1 onion, chopped

1 rib celery, chopped

1 cup seasoned stuffing mix

2 cups (480 ml) fat-free beef broth

1 tablespoon dry red wine

1 bay leaf

3 tablespoons *cold* water

2 tablespoons cornstarch

Freshly ground black pepper, garnish

Here I use a store-bought stuffing to minimize prep time and maximize flavor. It's a handy ingredient for those times when speed is essential.

MAKES 4 SERVINGS   **MEDIUM CROCKERY POT**

Using a meat mallet, pound the steaks to ¼ inch (6 mm) thick.

Coat a nonstick skillet with the cooking spray and heat over medium-high heat. Add the mushrooms, onions, and celery, and sauté, stirring, until the mushrooms and onions are lightly browned.

In a bowl, combine the mushroom mixture, stuffing mix, and ½ cup (120 ml) of the broth. Place a spoonful of the stuffing mixture in the center of each steak; roll up and fasten with a toothpick.

Heat the nonstick skillet again; add the roll-ups and cook until they're browned on all sides. Transfer to the crockery pot. Pour in the wine and the remaining ½ cup (120 ml) broth. Add the bay leaf. Cover and cook on LOW until the beef is cooked through and very tender, 6 to 8 hours.

Remove to a platter, reserving the broth; keep the beef warm. Discard the bay leaf. Pour the broth into a saucepan.

Combine the cornstarch and cold water in a measuring cup. Pour into the broth and cook, stirring, over medium heat until thickened, about 2 minutes. Serve the roll-ups with the thickened broth. Sprinkle the pepper over each serving.

PER SERVING: 243 calories, 4.7 g fat (18% of calories), 1.5 g saturated fat, 72 mg cholesterol, 296 mg sodium, 1.2 g dietary fiber.

QUICK TIP: Chop the mushrooms, onions, and celery fairly fine. Small pieces make it easier to roll up the stuffing and beef.

MUSHROOM-STUFFED BEEF ROLL-UPS

Fajitas with Cumin Seeds

½ pound (228 g) lean chip steak, cut into thin strips

¼ cup (60 ml) fat-free beef broth

2 medium onions, halved lengthwise and thinly sliced

1 medium sweet green or red pepper, thinly sliced

6 cloves garlic, minced

½ teaspoon cumin seeds

1 chili pepper, minced

½ cup (75 g) frozen corn

½ cup (114 g) cooked black beans

Juice of 1 lime

4 flour or corn tortillas (8-inch, 20 cm diameter)

4 tablespoons nonfat sour cream

½ cup (120 ml) medium or hot salsa

Sprigs of cilantro, for garnish

A lime-and-pepper marinade gives traditional steak fajitas their flavor and tenderness. Here, slow cooking achieves the same mouth-watering results.

MAKES 4 FAJITAS   **MEDIUM CROCKERY POT**

Combine the steak, broth, onions, sweet pepper, garlic, cumin, chili pepper, corn, and beans in a crockery pot. Cover and cook on LOW until the steak is tender, 7 to 9 hours. Stir in half the lime juice.

Divide the steak mixture among the tortillas; then roll them up. Place them in a microwave-safe baking dish and sprinkle them with the remaining lime juice. Warm everything in a microwave oven on high for 1 minute. To warm in a regular oven, cover with foil and place in a preheated oven for 5 minutes at 325°F (163°C). Top with the sour cream and salsa, and garnish with the cilantro.

PER FAJITA: About 377 calories, 9.3 g fat (22% of calories), 3.2 g saturated fat, 34 mg cholesterol, 378 mg sodium, 3 g dietary fiber.

COOK'S NOTE: Ground cumin is a perfectly acceptable replacement for cumin seeds. Use a little less, however.

Beef Stir-Fry with Black Bean Sauce

6 ounces (170 g) Thai rice noodles

1 tablespoon reduced-sodium soy sauce

2 tablespoons black bean sauce

1 tablespoon plus ¾ cup (180 ml) fat-free chicken broth

2 teaspoons peanut oil

1 cup (1 large onion) thinly sliced red onion wedges

1 small green bell pepper, cut into thin strips

About 10 ounces (284 g) shredded beef brisket (page 134)

1 cup ((100 g) coarsely chopped green cabbage, blanched for 1 minute

1 cup (340 g) small cauliflower florets, blanched for 1 minute

MAKES 4 SERVINGS

Cook the noodles according to package directions; drain. Combine the soy sauce, black bean sauce, and 1 tablespoon broth in a small bowl.

Heat the oil in a large nonstick skillet or wok over medium-high heat. Add the onions and pepper. Stir-fry for 2 minutes. Add the beef. Stir-fry for 2 minutes. Add the cabbage and cauliflower. Stir-fry for 2 minutes.

Stir in the soy-sauce mixture. Cover and cook for 2 minutes. Add the noodles, tossing to mix. Pour in the remaining chicken broth. Cover and cook for 1 minute. Serve immediately.

PER SERVING: 327 calories, 7.3 g fat, 312 mg sodium, 2.5 g dietary fiber.

FAJITAS WITH CUMIN SEEDS

Sagely Seasoned Pork Sirloin Roast

2¼ (540 ml) cups fat-free beef broth

¼ cup (60 ml) dry white wine

1 onion, chopped

½ red bell pepper, chopped

1 rib celery, chopped

1 clove garlic, minced

3-pound (1.36 kg) pork sirloin roast, trimmed of fat

2 teaspoons yellow mustard seeds

8 to 10 fresh sage leaves

1 cup (200 g) wild pecan rice

1 tablespoon pine nuts, toasted

Wonderfully subdued and slightly minty, sage plays a dual role in this recipe: It boostes flavor and keeps the roast moist at the same time. If you can't find fresh sage, try basil leaves or sprigs of rosemary.

MAKES 6 SERVINGS   **LARGE CROCKERY POT**

Combine broth, wine, onion, pepper, celery, and garlic in the crockery pot. Add the pork. Press the mustard seeds into the pork above the liquid. Arrange the sage over the mustard. Cover and cook on LOW until the pork is cooked through and a meat thermometer registers 160°F or 71.1°C, 8 to 10 hours. Let rest for 10 minutes before slicing and serving.

Meanwhile, cook the rice according to package directions. Add the nuts and toss to combine.

Divide the roast into thirds. Freeze two-thirds for later use. Slice the remaining roast and serve with the rice.

PER SERVING: 290 calories, 8.4 g fat, 126 mg sodium, 2.6 g dietary fiber.

QUICK TIP: Look for pine nuts under these names: pine nuts, Indian nuts, piñon nuts, pignoli, and pignolia.

Chinese Beef Balls with Bok Choy

¾ pound (340 g) ground sirloin

½ cup (40 g) quick oats

1 teaspoon five-spice powder

¼ cup (20 g) finely chopped bok choy leaves

1 egg white

1 tablespoon dried minced onions

2 teaspoons olive oil

1 can (14 ounces, 420 ml) fat-free beef broth

2 tablespoons black bean sauce

3 cups (240 g) bok choy stalks, sliced

8 ounces (228 g) rice sticks

Chinese chili sauce with garlic (optional)

These spice-infused meatballs have the power to please your palate. Five-spice powder provides the flavor kick while bok choy, rice sticks, and black bean sauce combine for a stylish accompaniment.

MAKES 4 SERVINGS   **MEDIUM CROCKERY POT**

Combine the beef, oats, five-spice powder, bok choy leaves, egg white, and onions in a large bowl. Form mixture into 1-inch (2.5 cm) beef balls. Heat the oil in a large nonstick skillet over medium-high heat. Add the meatballs and cook, turning occasionally, until lightly browned about 10 minutes.

Combine the broth, black bean sauce, and meatballs in the crockery pot. Cover and cook on LOW or HIGH until the meatballs are cooked through and the flavors are blended, 5 to 6 hours on LOW or 3 to 4 hours on HIGH. Stir in the bok choy. Cover and cook until tender, 10 to 15 minutes.

Cook the rice sticks according to package directions; drain well and divide among 4 plates. Spoon the beef mixture over the rice sticks. Serve with the chili sauce if desired.

PER SERVING: 304 calories, 9.2 g fat, 190 mg sodium, 3.5 g dietary fiber.

QUICK TIP: Rice sticks — similar to rice noodles except they are about ¼-inch (6 mm) wide — are available in the Asian section of most large supermarkets, as is Chinese black bean sauce.

Red- and Black-Bean Chili

1 pound (455 g) extra lean ground beef

6 cloves garlic, minced

3 large onions, chopped

2 large sweet green peppers, chopped

2 chili peppers, minced

1 can (28 ounces, 800 g) crushed tomatoes

1 cup (240 ml) water

4 cups home-cooked red kidney beans, or 2 cans (15 ounces, 426 g, each), rinsed and drained

2 cups home-cooked black beans, or 1 can (16 ounces, 455 g), rinsed and drained

3 tablespoons chili powder

1 teaspoon ground cumin

¼ teaspoon ground allspice

¼ teaspoon ground coriander

1 tablespoon red wine vinegar or cider vinegar

Perfect for fall and winter suppers, this spicy dish packs plenty of healthful fiber. Serve with carrot and celery crudités and crusty sourdough bread.

MAKES 8 SERVINGS   **LARGE CROCKERY POT**

Brown the beef in a nonstick skillet over medium-high heat, until the meat is browned and crumbly, about 3 minutes. Spoon off the fat as it accumulates. Add the garlic and onions, and cook until the onions are translucent, about 3 minutes.

Transfer the beef mixture to a crockery pot. Add the sweet peppers and chili peppers, tomatoes, water, red and black beans, chili powder, cumin, allspice, coriander, and vinegar. Cover and cook on LOW for 6 to 8 hours.

PER SERVING: About 353 calories, 8 g fat (20% of calories), 2.9 g saturated fat, 45 mg cholesterol, 243 mg sodium, 8.7 g dietary fiber.

COOK'S NOTE: This hearty chili tastes superb the second day. Store it in the refrigerator, and reheat it until hot and bubbly.

Savory Lamb Chops

1 can (14 ounces, 420 ml) fat-free
    beef broth

4 sprigs fresh mint

¾ pound (340 g) lamb shoulder chops,
    trimmed of fat

2 ounces (57 g) fresh chives, chopped

2 poblano chilies, seeded and chopped

¼ teaspoon freshly ground
    black pepper

1 tablespoon fresh rosemary leaves

¼ cup (36 g) precooked cornmeal (such
    as Masarepa®) or instant flour

1 teaspoon browning and
    seasoning sauce

An unusual threesome of mint, chilies, and rosemary jazzes up these lamb chops. The rich, spicy sauce that accompanies the chops is ideal for giving a sprightly twist to potatoes or noodles as well.

MAKES 4 SERVINGS　　　　　　　　**MEDIUM CROCKERY POT**

Combine the broth, mint, lamb, chives, chilies, black pepper, and rosemary in the crockery pot. Cover and cook on LOW or HIGH until the lamb is tender, 5 to 6 hours on LOW or 3 to 4 hours on HIGH.

Remove the lamb to a platter, reserving the cooking liquid, and cover with foil to keep warm. Skim fat from the reserved liquid. Stir in the cornmeal and browning sauce, and cook, stirring, until thickened. Serve over the chops.

PER SERVING: 237 calories, 10.2 g fat, 134 mg sodium, 1.5 g dietary fiber.

QUICK TIP: Precooked cornmeal and instant flour dissolve quickly and lump free in hot liquids.

Veal Cutlet Roulade

1 pound (455 g) veal cutlets, pounded to
    ¼ inch (6 mm) thick

4 Swiss chard leaves, stems removed

2 shallots, thinly sliced

½ teaspoon dried savory leaves

Kitchen string

Olive-flavored nonstick spray

½ cup (100 g) uncooked barley

½ cup (120 ml) fat-free chicken broth

½ cup (120 ml) water

1 tablespoon white wine vinegar

⅛ teaspoon white pepper

Freshly ground black pepper,
    for garnish

Snipped fresh chives, for garnish

In this dish, Swiss chard and shallots are wrapped in tender lean meat. The result: an entrée that's elegant enough for a sophisticated dinner, easy enough for every-night fare.

MAKES 4 SERVINGS　　　　　　　　**LARGE CROCKERY POT**

Place the veal on a work surface. Top each cutlet with some chard and shallots. Sprinkle with the savory. Roll up each cutlet; tie it closed with a piece of kitchen string.

Coat a nonstick skillet with the nonstick spray, and brown the veal roll on all sides over medium-high heat.

Combine the barley, broth, water, and vinegar in an electric crockery pot. Transfer the veal to the crockery pot; sprinkle with the white pepper. Cover and cook on LOW until the veal is tender, 7 to 9 hours.

Serve the veal with the barley; garnish the barley with the black pepper and chives.

PER SERVING: About 285 calories, 6.4 g fat (20% of calories), 1.7 g saturated fat, 99 mg cholesterol, 152 mg sodium, 3.6 g dietary fiber.

COOK'S NOTE: For variety, substitute spinach for the Swiss chard and small onions for the shallots.

SAVORY LAMB CHOPS

Just Desserts and Breads

Hot Cranberry Punch

1 quart (960 ml) apple juice

1 quart (960 ml) cranberry juice

6 whole cloves

4 lemon herbal tea bags

1 cinnamon stick

Lemon slices, for garnish

Cranberry flavor and color prevail in this spicy, not-too-sweet refresher. Ladle it hot into mugs garnished with lemon slices. Ummm! It's delightful.

MAKES 16 SERVINGS   **MEDIUM CROCKERY POT**

Pour the juices into the crockery pot. Add the cloves, tea, and cinnamon. Cover and cook on LOW until hot, about 3 hours.

Remove the cinnamon and tea bags. Ladle into mugs, and garnish each serving with a lemon slice.

PER SERVING: About 60 calories, 0.1 g fat (2% of calories), 0 g saturated fat, 0 mg cholesterol, 3 mg sodium, 0.1 g dietary fiber.

COOK'S NOTE: Substitute orange tea and slices for the lemon, if desired.

Heavenly Poached Pears

Juice of 1 lemon

1 cup (240 ml) water

8 slightly underripe Bartlett, Anjou, or Bosc pears, peeled

2 tablespoons crystallized ginger

2 teaspoons lemon peel

2 tablespoons white sugar

5 tablespoons brown sugar

1 teaspoon ground cinnamon

2 cups (480 ml) white grape juice

FOR THE ALMOND CREAM:

1 cup (240 g) plain low-fat yogurt

1 cup (240 g) nonfat sour cream

½ teaspoon almond extract

Topped with luscious ALMOND CREAM, these spicy pears make a grand finale worthy of the fanciest dinner party, but are easy to make.

MAKES 8 SERVINGS   **LARGE CROCKERY POT**

Place the lemon juice and water in a medium bowl; dip the pears into the lemon mixture to keep them from browning. Stand the pears up in a crockery pot.

Combine the ginger, 1 teaspoon of lemon peel, white sugar, 2 tablespoons of brown sugar, cinnamon, and grape juice in a measuring cup; pour the juice mixture over the pears. Cover and cook on LOW until the pears are tender, about 5 hours. Remove the pears from the heat and let them cool in the poaching liquid.

TO MAKE THE ALMOND CREAM: While the pears are cooking, drain the yogurt in a cheesecloth-lined strainer in the refrigerator. When ready to serve the pears, combine the drained yogurt (yogurt cheese), sour cream, remaining brown sugar, and almond extract; stir until well blended. Serve each pear with a dollop of almond cream; garnish with the remaining peel.

PER SERVING: About 212 calories, 0.7 g fat (3% of calories), 0 g saturated fat, 1 mg cholesterol, 42 mg sodium, 4.7 g dietary fiber.

Mocha Bread Pudding

4 tablespoons cocoa

1 cup (240 ml) hot coffee

1 egg

¼ cup (60 ml) fat-free egg substitute

2 cups (480 ml) low-fat (1%) milk

1 cup (240 ml) fat-free milk

½ cup (100 g) sugar

1 teaspoon vanilla

6 slices dry firm white bread, cubed

½ teaspoon ground cinnamon

Nonfat whipped topping (optional)

Hooked on chocolaty-coffee flavors? Then you'll adore this pudding. It's satisfyingly rich-tasting and, like most bread puddings, is best when made with a hearty country-style bread.

MAKES 6 SERVINGS   **MEDIUM CROCKERY POT**

Whisk the cocoa into the coffee in a small bowl or a 2-cup (480 ml) measure. Let cool.

While the coffee is cooling, lightly beat the egg and egg substitute in a large bowl. Stir in the coffee mixture, low-fat milk, fat-free milk, sugar, vanilla, and bread. Pour into the crockery pot. Sprinkle with the cinnamon.

Cover and cook on LOW until a knife inserted into the center of the pudding comes out clean, 2½ to 3½ hours. Serve warm, at room temperature or chilled. And top with the whipped topping if using.

PER SERVING: 192 calories, 2 g fat, 0 g saturated fat, 0 mg cholesterol, 215 mg sodium, 0.7 g dietary fiber.

QUICK TIP: Stored in a covered container in the refrigerator for up to 3 days.

Almond-Ginger-Peach Puree

2 cups (7 ounces, 185 g) dried peach halves

1 cup (56 g) dried apple slices

3 cups (720 ml) white grape juice

3 tablespoons sugar

2 tablespoons brown sugar

2 teaspoons minced crystallized ginger

1 cinnamon stick

½ teaspoon almond extract

An uncommonly rich sauce that's marvelous by itself or as a topping for angel food cake or frozen vanilla yogurt. For crunch, top the whole thing with a sprinkling of no-fat-added granola.

MAKES 16 SERVINGS   **MEDIUM CROCKERY POT**

Combine the peaches, apples, grape juice, sugars, ginger, and cinnamon in the crockery pot. Cover and cook on LOW until the peaches are very tender, 6 to 8 hours (on HIGH, 3½ to 5 hours). Discard the cinnamon and stir in the almond.

PER ¼ CUP: About 110 calories, 0.2 g fat (1% of calories), 0 g saturated fat, 0 mg cholesterol, 9 mg sodium, 2.3 g dietary fiber.

COOK'S NOTE: The sauce stores beautifully in the refrigerator for several days. To serve warm, heat briefly (5 to 15 seconds) in a microwave set on MEDIUM.

MOCHA BREAD PUDDING

Warm Fresh Fruit Delight

2 cups (300 g) white grapes

2 nectarines, peeled and sliced

2 Anjou pears, peeled and cubed

2 Golden Delicious apples, peeled and cubed

2 oranges, peeled and sectioned

1 stick cinnamon

¼ teaspoon ground nutmeg

1 cup (240 ml) orange juice

2 cups (480 g) low-fat vanilla yogurt, frozen low-fat vanilla yogurt, or orange sherbet

This delicate, refreshing dessert focuses on five favorite fruits: apples, pears, oranges, grapes, and nectarines. If juicy nectarines are elusive, use frozen peaches instead. The seasoning in this dish is subtle; if you want something spicier, add lemon juice and a dash of mace.

MAKES 6 SERVINGS   **MEDIUM CROCKERY POT**

Combine the grapes, nectarines, pears, apples, oranges, cinnamon, nutmeg, and orange juice in the crockery pot. Toss gently to mix. Cover and cook on LOW or HIGH just until the apples are tender, 3 to 3 hours on LOW or 1½ to 3 hours on HIGH.

Discard the cinnamon; stir to mix. Let cool slightly. Serve topped with the yogurt, frozen yogurt, or sherbet.

PER SERVING: 209 calories, 1.8 g fat, 54 mg sodium, 4.6 g dietary fiber.

QUICK TIP: Serve within 30 minutes of cooking; otherwise, the fruit will begin to darken.

Basic Wheat Dumplings

⅔ cup (95 g) unbleached flour

⅔ cup (95 g) whole wheat flour

2 teaspoons baking powder

⅔ cup (160 ml) skim milk

2 tablespoons canola oil

Complement your next stew with these quick-to-make steamed breads.

MAKES 8 DUMPLINGS   **LARGE CROCKERY POT**

Whisk the unbleached and whole wheat flours and baking powder together in a bowl.

In another bowl, mix the milk and the oil. Pour the liquid mixture into the flour mixture; stir with a fork until the ingredients are just combined.

Switch the heat to HIGH on the crockery pot filled with steaming stew. Drop 8 spoonfuls of dough in a single layer onto the stew. Cover and steam the dumplings until a toothpick inserted into the center of one comes out clean, about 30 minutes. To serve, top each dumpling with a generous serving of stew.

PER DUMPLING: About 112 calories, 3.8 g fat (30% of calories), 0.3 g saturated fat, 0 mg cholesterol, 15 mg sodium, 1.2 g dietary fiber.

COOK'S NOTE: For white dumplings, replace the whole wheat flour with unbleached flour.

Peach and Apple Compote

1 cup (92 g) dried peach halves

1 cup (56 g) dried apple slices

½ cup (80 g) golden raisins

½ cup (85 g) currants

1 cup (228 g) dried apricot halves

1 cinnamon stick

2½ cups (600 ml) water

Juice of 1 lemon

1 teaspoon grated lemon peel

1 tablespoon brown sugar

Frozen nonfat vanilla ice cream or
    yogurt (optional)

An after-dinner winner, this compote, which has nary a gram of fat, will surely satisfy your sweet tooth. It's great for breakfast and snacks, too.

MAKES 8 SERVINGS   **MEDIUM CROCKERY POT**

Combine the peaches, apples, raisins, currants, apricots, and cinnamon in the crockery pot. Stir in the water, lemon juice and peel, and sugar. Cover and cook on LOW until the fruit is tender, 5 to 7 hours. Discard the cinnamon stick. Serve with ice cream or yogurt, if you wish.

PER SERVING: About 150 calories, 0.2 g fat (1% of calories), 0 g saturated fat, 0 mg cholesterol, 13 mg sodium, 3.4 g dietary fiber.

COOK'S NOTES: Stir the cooked fruit gently. The compote keeps, covered, in the refrigerator for several days.

Walnut-Raisin-Apple Bake

½ cup (120 ml) apple cider

Juice of 1 lemon

2 teaspoons maple syrup

2 tablespoons raisins

1 tablespoon dark brown sugar

1 teaspoon ground cinnamon

1 teaspoon ground walnuts

4 large Macintosh apples, cored

Looking for a carefree, applicious dessert? This sweet treat will fill the bill. Serve it with your favorite nonfat frozen topping.

MAKES 4 APPLES   **LARGE RECTANGULAR CROCKERY POT**

Pour the cider, lemon juice, and maple syrup into the crockery pot.

Combine the raisins, sugar, cinnamon, and walnuts in a small bowl. Place the apples in the crockery pot. Using a spoon, fill the center of the apples with the raisin mixture. Cover and cook on LOW until the apples are tender, 2 to 3 hours.

PER APPLE: About 140 calories, 1.3 g fat (7% of calories), 0.1 g saturated fat, 0 mg cholesterol, 4.0 mg sodium, 3.4 g dietary fiber.

COOK'S NOTE: Like firm baked apples? Replace the Macintosh apples with Golden Delicious.

POACHED PEARS WITH RASPBERRY GLAZE

Poached Pears with Raspberry Glaze

6 cups (1.44 l) cran-raspberry
    juice cocktail

2 cups (480 ml) unsweetened
    apple juice

1 cinnamon stick

2 lemon or orange tea bags

4 firm Bosc or Anjou pears, peeled

¼ cup (60 ml) raspberry preserves,
    melted

Here, I offer a 3-D dessert: delightfully easy, delightfully attractive, delightfully delicious. Serving suggestion: Top the pears with a dollop of vanilla low-fat yogurt.

MAKES: 4 SERVINGS   **MEDIUM CROCKERY POT**

Combine the juices, cinnamon, tea bags, and pears in the crockery pot. Cover and cook on LOW or HIGH just until the pears are tender, 3 to 4 hours on LOW or 1½ to 3 hours on HIGH.

Discard the cinnamon stick and tea bags. Let the pears cool in the mulled juice. Using a slotted spoon, remove the pears to dessert plates, reserving the mulled juice for another time, and drizzle the pears with preserves. Serve immediately.

PER SERVING: 146 calories, 0.7 g fat (4% of calories), 0 g saturated fat, 0 mg cholesterol, 8 mg sodium, 4.2 g dietary fiber.

QUICK TIP: The reserved cinnamon-raspberry poaching juice from this recipe makes for a singular sweet-tart mulled beverage. To serve it as a mid-afternoon pick-me-up, simply warm the juice on the stove top or in the crockery pot. Serve it in mugs, and use additional cinnamon sticks as stirrers.

Bread Pudding with Raisins and Walnuts

1 egg

3 egg whites

2 cups (114 g) packed soft white
    bread cubes

3 cups (720 ml) skim milk

1 teaspoon light margarine

⅔ cups (130 g) sugar

½ teaspoon vanilla

½ cups (58 g) coarsely broken walnuts

½ cup (80 g) raisins

Nonfat whipped topping, for garnish

Custardy and rich-tasting, this dessert is a fresh version of the treat my mother used to make with "day-old" bread.

MAKES 8 SERVINGS   **MEDIUM CROCKERY POT**

Beat the egg and egg whites together in a large bowl. Mix in the bread, milk, margarine, sugar, vanilla, walnuts, and raisins. Pour the mixture into the crockery pot. Cover and cook on LOW until a knife inserted into the center of the pudding comes out clean, 2½ to 3½ hours. Serve warm or chilled, and garnish with the nonfat whipped topping.

PER SERVING: About 219 calories, 5.9 g fat (23% of calories), 0.7 g saturated fat, 28 mg cholesterol, 137 mg sodium, 1 g dietary fiber.

COOK'S NOTE: For more fiber, replace the white bread with whole wheat bread. You can keep this special treat in the refrigerator for up to 3 days.

Cinnamon-Spiced Apple Cider

3 Macintosh apples, peeled and
thinly sliced

2 quarts (1.9 l) apple cider or juice

2 cinnamon sticks

6 whole cloves

Whipped cream (optional)

Nutmeg (optional)

Cider and spice and everything nice! That's what this warming beverage is made of. Enjoy it for the holidays, during quiet times by the fire—anytime a soothing drink is in order.

MAKES 16 SERVINGS   **MEDIUM CROCKERY POT**

Place the apples in the crockery pot. Add the cider and the cinnamon. Cover and cook on LOW until the cider is hot and the apples are tender, about 4 hours. Serve mugfuls with slices of apple. Top with a dollop of cream and a pinch of nutmeg, if you wish.

PER SERVING: About 75 calories, 0.2 g fat (3% of calories), 0 g saturated fat, 0 mg cholesterol, 4 mg sodium, 0.5 g dietary fiber.

COOK'S NOTE: Serve with spoons so people can eat the apples.

Ginger-Poached Pears

4 firm Bosc pears, peeled, cored,
and halved

3 cups (720 ml) unsweetened
apple juice

¼ cups (60 ml) light rum

1 teaspoon chopped crystallized ginger

1 cinnamon stick

1 lemon, thinly sliced

There's nothing shy about these pears. During cooking, they soak up the sensational flavors of rum, cinnamon, and crystallized ginger and become subtly sweet yet slightly spicy. Serve them warm or at room temperature and top each half with a dollop of your favorite lemon sherbet.

MAKES 4 SERVINGS   **MEDIUM CROCKERY POT**

Arrange the pears in the crockery pot. Combine the juice, rum, and ginger, and pour over the pears. Add the cinnamon and arrange the lemon slices over the pears. Cover and cook on LOW or HIGH until the pears are very tender, 3 to 4 hours on LOW or 1½ to 3 hours on HIGH. Let cool slightly.

Serve the pears and poaching liquid warm or at room temperature, discarding the cinnamon stick and lemon slices.

PER SERVING: 315 calories, 1.3 g fat, 8 mg sodium, 5.6 g dietary fiber.

QUICK TIP: For best results, use slightly underripe pears.

Cranberry-Orange Pear Slices

1½ cups (495 g) jellied cranberry sauce

¼ cup (60 ml) orange juice

1 teaspoon orange peel

4 slightly underripe pears, peeled
and sliced

3 cups (720 g) nonfat vanilla ice cream

A scrumptious, chunky sauce for topping nonfat cakes and ice creams. Hostesses, note: This sauce is easily doubled, even tripled, to serve a crowd.

MAKES 6 SERVINGS   **LARGE CROCKERY POT**

Place sauce, juice, peel, and pears in the crockery pot. Cover and cook until the pears are tender, 6 to 8 hours. Serve warm over the ice cream.

PER SERVING: About 278 calories, 0.5 g fat (2% of calories), 0 g saturated fat, 0 mg cholesterol, 74 mg sodium, 3.9 g dietary fiber.

COOK'S NOTE: To make a pear puree, use fully ripe pears. After cooking, use a hand-held blender to puree the pears.

Hot Chocolate

4 cups (960 ml) skim or low-fat
(1%) milk

¼ cups (50 g) sugar

⅓ cup (115 g) chocolate-flavored syrup

Marshmallows, marshmallow creme, or
nonfat whipped topping

On a brisk day, enjoy a warm-you-up treat that's always a family favorite.

MAKES 5 SERVINGS   **MEDIUM CROCKERY POT**

Mix the milk, sugar, and syrup in the crockery pot. Cover and cook on LOW until the milk is hot, 2 to 3 hours. Stir, and ladle into mugs. Garnish with the marshmallows, marshmallow creme or whipped topping.

PER SERVING: About 131 calories, 0.5 g fat (3% of calories), 0.3 g saturated fat, 2.9 mg cholesterol, 94 mg sodium, 0 g dietary fiber.

COOK'S NOTE: If you're in a hurry for hot milk, heat it on HIGH for an hour; then turn the crockery pot to LOW. Left on HIGH, the milk might scorch.

Light Swedish Rice Pudding

4 cups (960 ml) skim milk

¼ cups (50 g) medium-grain rice

½ cups (100 g) sugar

½ teaspoon ground cardamom

½ teaspoon vanilla

½ cups (120 g) vanilla nonfat yogurt

Cinnamon-sugar, for garnish

This no-fuss, cardamom-spiced dessert is comfort food at its very best.

MAKES 6 SERVINGS　　　　　**MEDIUM CROCKERY POT**

Mix the milk, rice, sugar, and cardamom in the crockery pot. Cover and cook on LOW until the rice is very soft, 7 to 8 hours. Remove the rice from the crockery pot, and stir in the vanilla. Let cool at room temperature for about 1 hour; stir in the yogurt. Chill until cold, at least 4 hours. Garnish each serving with the cinnamon-sugar.

PER SERVING: About 156 calories, 0.3 g fat (2% of calories), 0.2 g saturated fat, 2.7 mg cholesterol, 102 mg sodium, 0 g dietary fiber.

COOK'S NOTE: To increase the fiber in this old-fashioned pudding, replace the white rice with brown rice, and add a hnadful of raisins when you remove the bowl from the heat.

Pumpkin Pudding

1 egg

2 egg whites

1½ cup (680 g) canned or home-cooked
　　pureed pumpkin

2 cans (12 ounces, 360 ml, each)
　　evaporated skim milk

1 teaspoon light margarine

⅓ cup (160 g) brown sugar

⅓ cup (67 g) white sugar

1 teaspoon ground cinnamon

½ teaspoon ground allspice

½ teaspoon ground nutmeg

½ cup raisins or chopped dates

2 cups packed soft bread cubes

1½ (360 g) cups brandied yogurt
　　topping

FOR BRANDIED YOGURT TOPPING:

2 cups (485 g) low-fat vanilla yogurt

Cheesecloth

1 teaspoon brandy extract

An old-fashioned custardy pudding that'll evoke fond memories of holiday desserts. The best part: It's nutritious and delicious.

MAKES 8 SERVINGS　　　　　**MEDIUM CROCKERY POT**

Beat the egg and egg whites together until they're a light lemon color. Combine the eggs, pumpkin, milk, and margarine in the crockery pot. Stir in the sugars, cinnamon, allspice, nutmeg, raisins or dates, and bread cubes. Cover and cook on LOW until a knife inserted in the center of the pudding comes out clean, 5½ to 7½ hours.

PER SERVING: About 232 calories, 1.5 g fat (6% of calories), 0.5 g saturated fat, 30 mg cholesterol, 206 mg sodium, 2.1 g dietary fiber.

COOK'S NOTE: To make brandied yogurt topping, place 2 cups (485 g) low-fat vanilla yogurt in a cheesecloth-lined strainer or colander. Let it drain in the refrigerator while the pudding is cooking. Stir 1 teaspoon brandy extract into the drained yogurt.

MIXED FRUIT COMPOTE

Mixed Fruit Compote

3 cups (720 ml) unsweetened
    apple juice

1 package (8 ounces, 228 g) mixed
    dried fruit

¾ cup (120 g) raisins

1 orange, sectioned and chopped

3 strips (about 2 x 3 inches, 5 cm x 7.5
    cm, each) orange peel

½ cup (120 ml) dry, fruity white wine,
    such as Riesling

1 stick cinnamon

2 whole cloves

Most cooks have a favorite dried fruit compote recipe. Here's mine. It's a tasty combination that's ideal for breakfast, brunch, or dessert. Dry white wine, orange peel, cinnamon, and cloves tone down the dried fruit's sweetness.

MAKES 4 SERVINGS　　　　　　　　　　**MEDIUM CROCKERY POT**

Combine the juice, dried fruit, raisins, orange sections, orange peel, wine, cinnamon, and cloves in the crockery pot. Cover and cook on LOW or HIGH until the dried fruit are tender, 3 to 4 hours on LOW or 1½ to 3 hours on HIGH. Let cool slightly.

Serve the fruit and poaching liquid warm or at room temperature, discarding the cinnamon stick and orange peel.

PER SERVING: 360 calories, 0.7 g fat, 15 mg sodium, 6.8 g dietary fiber.

QUICK TIP: When cutting orange peel, take care not to cut deeply into the white part (pith); it tastes bitter.

Quick Compote of Pears, Apricots and Cherries

6 ounces (170 g) dried pears

6 ounces (170 g) dried apricots

½ cup (80 g) dried cherries

½ cup (80 g) dried cranberries

2½ cups (600 ml) cranberry juice

1 lime, sliced

1 cinnamon stick

⅛-inch-thick (3 mm thick) slice
    of gingerroot

Somewhat tart and very satisfying, this dried fruit compote marries well with fruit sherbet or frozen yogurt.

MAKES: 6 SERVINGS　　　　　　　　　　**MEDIUM CROCKERY POT**

Combine pears, apricots, cherries, cranberries and cranberry juice, lime slices, cinnamon stick and gingerroot in the crockery pot. Cover and cook on LOW or HIGH until the fruits are tender, 3 to 4 hours on LOW or 1½ to 3 hours on HIGH.

Discard the cinnamon stick, lime slices, and gingerroot. Let cool. Serve the fruit warm or chilled.

PER SERVING: 237 calories, 0.7 g fat (3% of calories), 0 g saturated fat, 0 mg cholesterol, 9.3 mg sodium, 5.3 g dietary fiber.

QUICK TIP: Be sure to peel the gingerroot before adding it to the fruit mixture.

Culinary Math

Quick, quick! A creamy soup recipe calls for 1 cup of broccoli florets. How many pounds of fresh broccoli should you buy? A stew requires 2 cups of beef broth. How many cans should you open? Stumped? That's understandable. After all, who among us memorizes such nitty-gritty food facts? For an approximate answer (it's impossible to be exact), look to this concise table.

A   **Almonds, shelled, blanched**: ½ pound = 1½ cups whole = 2 cups slivered

Apples: 1 pound = 3 medium = 2¾ to 3 cups chopped or sliced

Apricots, dried: 1 pound = 2¾ cups = 4½ to 5½ cups cooked

Asparagus, fresh: 1 pound = 16 to 20 spears

Asparagus, frozen, cut: 1 package (10 ounces) = 2 cups

B   **Bananas**: 1 pound = 3 to 4 medium = 2 cups sliced = 1¾ cups mashed

Beans, green, fresh: 1 pound = 3½ cups whole

Beans, green, frozen: 1 package (9 ounces) = 1½ cups

Beans, kidney, canned: 16 to 17 ounces = 2 cups

Beans, kidney, dried: 1 pound = 2½ cups = 5½ cups cooked

Beans, navy, dried: 1 pound = 2⅓ cups = 5½ cups cooked

Beef broth: 1 can (14 ounces) = 1¾ cups

Beef, cooked, cubed: 1 cup = 6 ounces

Beef, ground: 1 pound = 2 cups uncooked

Beets, fresh, without tops: 1 pound = 2 cups chopped

Bread: 1 slice fresh = ½ cup soft crumbs = ¼ to ⅓ cup dry crumbs

Broccoli, fresh: 1 pound = 2 cups chopped

Broccoli, frozen: 1 package (10 ounces) = ½ cups chopped

Brussels sprouts, fresh: 1 pound = 4 cups

C   **Cabbage**: 1 pound = 3½ to 4½ cups shredded = 2 cups cooked

Carrots, fresh: 1 pound without tops = 3 cups chopped or sliced = 2½ to 3 cups shredded; 1 medium = ½ cup chopped or sliced

Carrots, frozen: 1 package (1 pound) = 2½ to 3 cups sliced

Cauliflower: 1 pound = 1½ cups small florets

Celery: 1 stalk = ½ cup chopped or sliced

Cheese—blue, feta, gorgonzola: 4 ounces = 1 cup crumbled

Cheese—cheddar, Monterey Jack: 1 pound = 4 cups shredded or grated

Cheese—Parmesan, Romano: 4 ounces = 1 cup shredded or grated

Chicken, cooked, cubed: 1 cup = 6 ounces

Chicken broth: 1 can (14 ounces) = 1¾ cups

Corn, fresh: 2 to 3 ears = 1 cup kernels

Corn, frozen: 1 package (10 ounces) = 1¾ cups kernels

Cornmeal: 1 pound dry = 3 cups uncooked = 12 cups cooked

E   **Egg, large**: 1 yolk = 1 tablespoon; 1 white = 2 tablespoons

Egg, large: 7 to 8 = 1 cup

Eggplant: 1 pound = 3 to 4 cups diced

Egg substitute: ¼ cup = 1 whole egg; 1 package (8 ounces) = 1 cup = 4 whole eggs

G   **Garlic**: 2 medium cloves = 1 teaspoon minced

H   **Herbs—basil, cilantro, dill, parsley, thyme**: 1 tablespoon, fresh, chopped = 1 teaspoon dried

L   **Lemon**: 1 medium = 2 to 3 teaspoons grated peel and 3 tablespoons juice;
1 pound = 4 to 6 medium lemons = 1 cup juice

Lime: 1 medium = 1 teaspoon grated peel and 2 tablespoons juice;
1 pound = 6 to 8 medium limes = ⅓ to ⅔ cup juice

M   **Macaroni**: 1 pound = 4 cups dry = 8 cups cooked

Mushrooms, fresh: ½ pound = 2½ to 3 cups sliced = 1 cup sliced sautéed

N   **Noodles**: 1 pound = 6 cups dry = 7 cups cooked

O   **Okra, fresh**: 1 pound = 2 cups sliced

Onion: 1 medium = ½ cup minced = ¾ to 1 cup chopped

Orange: 1 medium = 2 tablespoons grated peel and ⅓ cup juice; 1 pound = 3 medium = 1 cup juice

P   **Parsnips**: 1 pound = 4 medium = 2 cups chopped

Peas, frozen: 1 package (10 ounces) = 2 cups

Peas, in pod: 1 pound = 1 to 1½ cups shelled

Peppers: 1 medium sweet = 1 cup chopped

Potatoes, sweet: 1 pound = 3 medium = 3½ to 4 cups cubed or sliced = 2 cups mashed

Potatoes, white: 1 pound = 3 medium = 3½ to 4 cups cubed or sliced = 2 cups mashed

R   **Rice, brown**: 1 cup uncooked = 4 cups cooked

Rice, white: 1 cup uncooked = 3 cups cooked

S   **Scallions**: 2 medium, white part only = 1 tablespoon

Scallions: 2 medium with green tops = ¼ cup

Spinach, fresh: 1 pound = 8 to 10 cups torn

Squash, yellow or zucchini: 1 pound = 3 medium = 2½ cups sliced

Squash, winter: 1 pound = 1 cup mashed

T   **Tomato, fresh**: 1 medium = ½ cup chopped; 1 pound = 3 large = 4 medium = 1½ cups chopped

Tomatoes, canned: 1 can (28 ounces) crushed = 3¾ cups

Y   **Yogurt**: ½ pint = 1 cup = 8 ounces

Emergency Substitutes

Uh-oh, you've checked the pantry and looked in the refrigerator, so there's no doubt about it: you're out of nonfat sour cream, Italian herb seasoning and chili powder. Three ingredients your favorite recipe calls for, and you planned to serve the recipe tonight. What now? Check this handy table; it'll help you find quick replacements for missing items. Just remember, the substitutes may give the recipe a somewhat different flavor or texture.

Recipe Requires	Quick Substitute
Bacon (1 slice crumbled)	Bacon bits (1 T)
Allspice	Cinnamon; dash of nutmeg
Bread crumbs, dry (1 cup)	Cracker crumbs (¾ cup)
Broth, beef or chicken (1 cup)	Bouillon cube (1) plus boiling water (1 cup)
Chili powder (1 T)	Hot-pepper sauce (a drop or two) plus oregano (¼ tsp) and cumin (¼ tsp)
Cinnamon (1 tsp)	Allspice (¼ tsp) or nutmeg (¼ tsp)
Cornstarch (1 T)	All-purpose flour (2 T)
Cumin (1 tsp)	Chili powder (1 tsp)
Egg (1 whole)	Egg substitute (¼ tsp)
Flour, as thickener (2 T)	Cornstarch (1 T) or quick-cooking tapioca (2 T)
Garlic (1 clove)	Garlic powder (⅛ tsp)
Ginger (1 tsp)	Allspice (½ tsp), cinnamon (1 tsp), or nutmeg (½ tsp)
Italian herb seasoning (1 tsp)	Basil, dried (1 tsp) plus thyme, dried leaves (1 tsp)
Lemon juice (1 tsp)	Cider vinegar (½ tsp)
Lemon peel (1 tsp grated)	Lemon extract (½ tsp)
Mustard, dry (1 tsp)	Mustard, prepared (1 T)
Nonfat sour cream (1 cup)	Plain nonfat yogurt (1 cup)
Onion (1 minced)	Onions, dried, minced (1 T)
Pumpkin pie spice	Cinnamon, ground (1 tsp) plus nutmeg, ground (½ tsp) and powdered ginger (½ tsp)
Seasoned bread crumbs, dry (1 cup)	Plain dry bread crumbs (⅞ cup) plus (1 cup) grated Parmesan cheese (1 T) and dried parsley (1 T)
Sherry (1 T)	Sherry extract (1 T)
Teriyaki sauce (1 T)	Soy sauce (1 T) plus powdered garlic (⅛ tsp) and minced fresh ginger (¼ tsp)
Tomato sauce (1 cup)	Tomato paste (½ cup) plus water (½ cup)
Vinegar (1 tsp)	Lemon juice (2 tsp)

Key to abbreviations: T = tablespoon; tsp = teaspoon

What Equals a Serving?

Bread, Cereal, Rice and Pasta Group:

- 1 slice of bread
- 1 ounce of ready-to-eat cereal
- ½ cup of cooked cereal, rice or pasta

Vegetable Group:

- 1 cup of raw leafy vegetables
- ½ cup of other vegetables—cooked or raw—chopped
- ½ cup of vegetable juice

Fruit Group:

- 1 medium apple, banana, orange
- ½ cup of chopped, cooked or canned fruit
- ½ cup of fruit juice

Milk Group:

- 1 cup of milk or yogurt
- 1½ ounces of natural cheese
- 2 ounces of processed cheese

Meat, Poultry, Fish, Dry Beans, Eggs, and Nuts Group:

- 2–3 ounces of cooked lean meat, poultry, or fish
- ½ cup of cooked dry beans or 1 egg counts as 1 ounce of lean meat. Two tablespoons of peanut butter or ⅓ cup of nuts counts as 1 ounce of meat.

Culinary Abbreviations

t = tsp = teaspoon

T = tbsp = tablespoon

c = cup

oz = ounce

fl oz = fluid ounce

lb = pound

g = gram

kg = kilogram

mg = milligram

L = liter

ml = milliliter

F = Fahrenheit

C = Celcius

Index